GW00865421

Enough is Enough

Enough is Enough

Billy Ray Wilson

authorHOUSE®

AuthorHouse™
1663 Liberty Drive
Bloomington, IN 47403
www.authorhouse.com
Phone: 1-800-839-8640

First published by AuthorHouse 12/7/2009

ISBN: 978-1-4490-5692-6 (e)
ISBN: 978-1-4490-5691-9 (sc)
ISBN: 978-1-4490-5690-2 (hc)

Library of Congress Control Number: 2009913000

Printed in the United States of America
Bloomington, Indiana

This book is printed on acid-free paper.

GLOSSARY

Foreword

A couple of years past, I published this book without the benefit of recently released information regarding our country's secret air war in the Kingdom of Laos, and supporting military installations in the Kingdom of Thailand. It was my hope, the book would create dissent in the civilian communities based upon my thirty five years of employment in agencies of the United States Government. I was wrong.

Now, as a 90% Permanent and Total Disabled military veteran, I've had years to reflect my life's ups and downs. What I have accepted is that I owe my sincere thanks and apologies to my past commanders, former employers, managers, supervisors, fellow military personnel, civilian counterparts that I worked with at overt and convert employment assignments.

And, at the international assignments, there were times, I admit, that I came across as the Ugly American. My stupidity was not based on racial or nationality prejudice, but the indigenous of the countries assigned did not have the work ethnic, as did many fellow Americans. However, by my retirement date, I believe that it was I that was the cause of the irritation.

My strict, ill-informed religious background created some turmoil beginning at my post-basic training air base at Homestead, Florida. I would refrain from joining my fellow airman at first when their actions did not conform with my religious teachings.

In particular, I remember a fellow Airman named, I believe, Joseph McGowan from Chester, Pennsylvania told me that my usage of such words as dog gone it, dad burn it, and similar Kentucky phrases were no different in context than saying shit, and the other words one heard around the barracks. McGowan was a practicing Catholic. I don't recall ever going to church on my free will just to hear a minister at Homestead Air Force Base, Florida.

With regards to tobacco and alcoholic beverages, I had never tried either one before the Homestead assignment. In basic training, when given box lunches, there were always a pack of Camels , or some other brand in the box. I never started. I did try a cigar and passed out. As far as alcohol in basic training, we never had liberty during my training period, so I never had opportunity to hit the night life in San Antonio, Texas. Naturally, I was subjected to alcohol in the barracks given to me by older Airman.

Basic training was an eye opener for me. I had never associated with individuals of color, my own age, prior to joining the air force. There were three Airman to a room, but the flight shared a common bathroom. Over the next six to eight weeks (I don't remember exactly), there were never any racial problems in our barracks or flight.

I was a virgin when I arrived at Homestead. (As I wrote above, I didn't get to San Antonio or into Mexico during my tour at Lackland Air Force Base, Texas.) My first sexual experience was with a prostitute in her forties in San Antonio, Texas during a temporary duty assignment to Lackland Air Force Base. Back at Homestead, my first wife seduced me (willingly, I might add). She told me she was pregnant so I had to get married. (My mother would have been extremely angry if I had not married.)

My first assignment with other nationalities was at Kunsan Air Base, Republic of South Korea. Men and women shared the same WC (bathroom). A real eye opener. I wrote my mother that I thought we lived in poverty, but we were rich by the standards I observed Korea.

Although, I never attended church services on my own unless it was a mandatory call, I still called myself a Christian. In Thailand and Laos, I wore a Buddha around my neck. My second wife, a Catholic, gave me a religious figurine, which I still own. In Saudi Arabia, I scanned over an English Version of the Koran but, in my mind, you could see where the text was plagiarized from either the Torah or Bible, possibly both.

My military life, physical and mental status remained constant (with the exception of a bad car accident, a divorce, and a divorce), until my assignment to Attache's Office, U.S. Embassy, Vientiane, Kingdom of Laos. Living on the economy with the population being Laotian, Moung, Thai, Cambodian, Vietnamese, French, and, of course, the diplomatic community to include the legal and illegal. I was one of the illegal.

At my assignment, I taught Royal Laotian Air Force Officers and Non-Commissioned Officers, worked with Laotian government officials and traveled to every Laotian fixed site where sheep dipped and/or temporary duty enlisted and pilot officers resided and/or worked. My mode of travel was via Air America, Continental, Bird & Son, Royal Laotian fixed wing aircraft and the Air Attache's C-47 aircraft (A door or window would open in the bottom of the aircraft to allow photographs to be taken of targets in which the Defense Intelligence Agency and/or Laotian Government may be interested).

For those not familiar, Laos was considered a hostile environment. From the time you crossed over the Mekong River from Thailand into Laos, you were subject to be fired upon and/or encounter hostile acts if landing in an unfriendly area (In Northern and Northeastern Thailand plus the Kingdom of Laos there were provinces and/or areas where Communist controlled or Communist contested).

In March 1968, a USAF TACAN site, manned by sheep dipped Air Force personnel and Thais. The site was over-run and 13 Americans killed. One of the individuals killed is scheduled or has been awarded the U.S. Congressional Medal of Honor (Sheep dipped means: you entered Laos as a civilian. All military Identification were taken. You were called Mister instead of your rank).

Other American team members were from the U.S. State Department, Central Intelligence Agency, USAID (United States Aid to Laos), Combined Air Support, and the U.S. Defense Attaches assigned to the U.S. Embassy. I was attached to the U.S. Air Attache (AIRA).

It is true over the period of assignment, our country was responsible for dropping more ordinance on the Kingdom of Laos as we did against German occupied Europe during World War II. However, in all fairness, during the years the American team was at it's greatest, the U.S. brought the Kingdom of Laos into the 20th Century.

With living on the economy and having a Thai girlfriend (mother of my son), I had the additional opportunity of hearing from non-government officials at to their desires and complaints. To the person, regardless of nationality (Vietnamese, Thai, Lao, Lao Moung), they did not care the name of their government whether Communist, Royal, or Democratic. They wanted to have the opportunity to get married, raise a family, receive an education, earn an income and travel at will. They wanted the same as we Americans take for granted.

Prior to arriving in Laos, I was one of those that was brainwashed by our government that if we did not stop the Communist in South Vietnam, then Southeast Asia would end up Communist. Well, Southeast Asia did end up being dominated economically by the powerful Communist state of China.

Military in Laos, CIA directed forces and U.S. Tactical and Strategic Air Resources allowed the government of Prime Minister Soucanna

Phouma to avoid Communist domination for at least five years. These years saw thousands of North Vietnamese, Laotian, Muong, Chinese, South Vietnamese, Thais, and Americans die for naught. Non-Communist forces did have some major short term victories. These victories taught us that we were not fighting just North Vietnam but China, Cuba, North Korea, and Russia. A lesson learned.

Sadly, I had to many days of involvement in Search and Rescue operations for pilots shot down, and calling in air resources to prevent a site from being over-run. Not all was sad, I was instrumental in assisting three former American Prisoners of War released by North Vietnam to speak with their family members, and provide them funds to purchase gifts for their family or friends prior to departing Laos for the United States.

Earlier, I identified that I fathered a son out of wedlock. With tremendous difficulty that included assistance from the late U.S. Senator and U.S. Ambassador to East Germany, the honorable John Sherman Cooper, (R-KY) my son born on August 17, 1970 is now a father of two. He resides in London, KY, as do I.

My son and I departed Laos during the first two weeks of January 1973 for Detroit, Michigan (An Aunt agreed to care for my son while I remained in the Air Force). I received an assignment to Wurtsmith Air Force Base, Oscoda, Michigan. At the air base, I was lucky to have one of the most outstanding Director of Operations and Operations Officers and, an equally outstanding Base Commander. Without these honorable men's understanding I would probably have failed in life.

At Wurtsmith, I learned the Department of Defense was forming a Joint U.S. Military Command called the Joint Casualty Resolution Center (JCRC) to recover the remains of U.S. Missing In Action (MIA) from the Vietnam War, and/ or attempt to resolve their status from reviewing classified documents, and other material received from a variety of international sources. I volunteered for an assignment to JCRC, as I was one of the persons speaking with the Search and Rescue On-Scene Commander or whatever agency or person providing details, as to the status of the MIA or KIA.

After six months or so at the organization, I wrote the Commander requesting to be either reassigned or discharged, as I would not remain at the command. The Command was political. There was little true effort to resolve MIA status. We were getting military personnel killed and wounded to collect bones or provide the Commander for a current recovery mission to brief at The Pentagon. I was re-assigned to Pease Air Force Base, New Hampshire.

A few years after returning from JCRC, I was married. I found a woman that I felt comfortable with, and thought she would be an excellent mother for my son. (Big Mistake) However, in all fairness, I was much to blame. I was no longer the person I was prior to going to Laos in 1968, nor was I the same person as the last years of my Air Force career. I was physically and mentally ill.

After retirement, I had a number of outstanding employment positions, but my physical and mental state would always come in to play. My last employer, the Department of Veteran affairs, Louisville Veteran Administration Medical Center medically retired me in 1998. The diagnosis' were: Post Traumatic Stress Disorder and Chronic Depression.

War is a terrible event which makes it a matter of necessity that Americans replace those in Congress of The United States, that allow the President of The United States of America to invade a sovereign nation on a religious crusade, or to benefit an American Manufacturing Corporation.

Family Origins

The United States of America is a country made by regrettably killing the Native Americans, relocating the Cherokee Nation from the East Coast of the United States to the Oklahoma Territory, and permitting slavery to remain active after the people declared the United States a sovereign nation. A nation, I might add, based on equality of every citizen regardless of their race, religion, creed, or point of origin.

We Americans, began our journey when a group of colonist decided our colonies would no longer cower to the English Crown. Based upon there decision, the Declaration of Independence was written and announced to the colonist, and to the King of England. Following the announcement and defeat of King George's mighty military, with the help of the French Navy and Army, our founders came forth with the United States Constitution.

The United States Constitution is the foundation of our country. The Founders wrote our government would consist of three separate branches - the Legislative, Executive, and Judicial. Each branch would have separate functions, but together would assure the country would not become a monarchy.

The Legislative Branch is the ultimate power of the American system. The Executive Branch is the government's administrative branch under the stewardship of The President of The United States and his cabinet. The Judicial Branch is supposed to monitor the activities of the other two branches, to assure they do not exceed their authority based on the U.S. Constitution.

Regarding the Supreme Court, it is my opinion, the Justices failed our nation in two extremely important cases before the court: (1) Allegedly, the Supreme Court informed President Andrew Jackson he did not have the authority, and his actions were in violation of the Constitution by his orders of moving the Cherokees to Oklahoma. Jackson was said to have announced "The Supreme Court does not have an army." (2) Siding with George W. Bush against Vice President Albert Gore in the 2000 national election. The Supreme Court Justices made George W. Bush the 43rd President of The United States Of America.

You may think I am getting away from the subject, but I am not.

Growing up in southern Kentucky part of Kentucky's 5th U.S. congressional District, known throughout many circles as the POT (marijuana) capitol of the United States, and per capita, the largest number of government subsidized citizens, I heard from different family members on both my father and mother's side, that we were of Native American blood.

I began the research which continues to date but learned, with some questions still outstanding: the Brown - Chandler and Wilson - Casteel families were indeed of indigenous blood. To this end even without the American Indian ancestry, I can be called a Melting Pot citizen without question.

My family tree's trunk consists of the Brown, Casteel, Chandler, and Wilson families. However, without the below listed families I would not be writing this autobiography:

Blevin (Blevins)	Black	Carter
Dees	Dobkins	George
Hamilton	Mershon	Moore
Pennington	Tackett	

The Brown family according to a number of different sources are from the native tribes in New England from the time of arrivals at Plymouth Rock, of more recent history, one of my great - grandfathers married a Mary "Polly" Tackett. She was born in Hawkins, TN which is a known county for American Indians.

Wilson family is truly mixed with many races and ethnic groups. Grandmother Lucy Wilson was a Casteel at birth. Her father was more Indian than white (The first Casteel, in Kentucky, allegedly married a full blooded American Indian who resided in an Indian settlement near a British Fort in Rockcastle County. Not all the Casteel family agrees with me and a large number of other family members regarding Indian blood).

The chandler Family had indigenous blood from both sides. Grandfather Chandler married a lady named Louisa Blevin and/ or Blevins. One of her fore parents was a Dobkins.

Of note, my research revealed history that I had never knew. For example, there were family members whose ancestry included Arabs and Arab Jews who were expelled from Spain by Queen Isabella (Queen Isabella's army defeated the Muslims who had conquered Spain and much of Europe during Prophet Mohammed's religious war). The Muslims/ non-Muslims were forced aboard ships bound to North America and discharged off of the coast of the present day Carolinas. From shore side, they traveled into the mountain range and lived among the American Indians.

The research concluded my ancestry consisted of: Europeans, North American Indians, North Africa, and East Asia. During a down period in research, I sent a DNA sample to the Gene Tree DNA Company in Utah to determine where our family originated (The test was based on my father's DNA. My mother's family were in the North America longer and their Indian heritage was greater. At a later date, I plan on checking my

DNA from my mother's side. Too expensive at present.). The following DNA data is provided:

European ancestry is close to ninety percent. The remaining leads us to the Native American, Sub-Sahara Africa and East Asia. We know the Wilson clan came from Ireland. The Brown family from Great Britain. Other family members came from France, Germany, Normand, East Asia, and the continent of Africa.

During the month of May 2009, I submitted another swab to an Ancestry Agency, again in Utah, to obtain the results of my father's "Y" Chromosome. For example: "starting from the point in human history when many ancient ancestral groups migrated out of Africa, discrete populations began to settle in different parts of the world. Over generations, as they adapted to their unique environments, each population's genes became slightly different from the original African Group. Some of the differences were random, while others provided genes for the characteristics which let groups thrive in their environments. Taken together those genetic differences define haplography." (One's grouping).

The Wilson Grouping belongs to haplography R1b, the Artisans, who first arrived in Europe from West Asia about 35,000 - 40,000 years ago. A sub-group of the Artisans, is associated with the Cro-Magnons. About 70% of individuals currently residing in Southern England are members of the Artisans. Other members can be found at high rates in the modern day populations of Spain, Portugal, France, Wales, Scotland, and Ireland.

To date, ancestry has provided me with 250 matches of my "Y" Chromosome from Thailand, Ireland, Great Britain, Australia (Allen Wilson), and throughout the United States. Truly Amazing.

What I have written in this autobiography may offend some families, as they may not agree with my personal life and beliefs, but my findings were without malice. Regrettably, in my opinion, in our findings, we found the European male acquired wives without regard to race, religion, ethnic group, etc. which was outstanding. However, as it is the case in some societies today, a female could be purchased, bartered, or stolen without the love one should seek between a man and his wife. I truly hope my male family members loved their wives not just demand sex, a housekeeper, servant, etc. Our family truly assimilated into the population.

Pre-Military Years

I was born in East Bernstadt, Laurel County, Kentucky, the United States of America during the early morning hours of September 21, 1943, the son of Raleigh Lee Wilson and Abbie Brown. The place of birth was at the home of my father's half-sister, Eva Moore, as very few rural Kentuckians were born in a hospital. My father had enlisted in the U.S. Marine Corps on December 9, 1942, completed basic training, and was on a ship with his Division to retake the Pacific Islands from the Japanese. My mother was a housewife, with a daughter, born on May 21, 1941, and now me to care for without a husband.

At the time of enlistment into the Marine Corps, my father was employed by Allis-Chambers, located in Norwood, OH. He returned to Allis-Chambers following his discharge from the Marine Corps.

Speaking of fathers, we draw our family name from our fathers, but to me, it is the mothers that deserve the credit for being there throughout one's life, in the good and the bad. For example, like today with many fathers away at war, it is the mother that bears the heaviest burden for the illegal on-going wars in Iraq and Afghanistan. To make matters worse, state governments have comprised with the Federal Government for their National Guard (militia) units to be included as part of the Department of Defense's active duty military in the Middle East. This scenario places the military dependents in the hands of parents or designated guardians which results, in my opinion, in mental stress to the dependents.

As a rural Kentuckian, our home environment was austere, family ties were strong, patriotism was alive and individual integrity was commonplace. At home, we were taught the history of our families, and the relationships with other families that made up our family tree. Likewise, we were taught our nation's history was not flawless, but the best country in the world's history. (Without a doubt, our country had periods and do so today that were/are ethically wrong and against the laws of the United States).

In Laurel County, which is in Southeast Kentucky, at the time of my student years, our education system was fiscally based on an agriculture economy. Naturally, the agriculture based economy created educational inequality for Kentucky's Fifth U.S. Congressional District. The Central and Northern areas of the state had multiple economic bases from manufacturing, tourism, and of course, agriculture. Today, the state's educational system is financed in part by Kentucky's State Lottery and taxes from property, vehicle tags & registration, and a small tax charge is billed on just about every non-government service used.

An example of the disparity between the Northern schools and those in Laurel County became apparent when I was a Junior at Hazel Green High School, Hazel Green, Kentucky. There was to be a state math contest at Georgetown College in Central Kentucky, where all high schools were represented. Hazel Green sent a team, of which I was a member. We learned first hand, the greater emphasis on math by the industrial based school systems. We were embarrassed.

Education in Southeastern Kentucky did not end at the public school, but continued throughout the year, year after year. However, the continuous education was religiously handed down from one generation to another, and too often administered to church goers by individuals seeking additional income, swindlers, and individuals without integrity.

Hold on! I probably hit a nerve when I wrote ministers without integrity. What I am saying is that to an educated, non-brainwashed person, such as, for example: Noah's Flood, plagues in Egypt, and Jews fleeing Egypt. Let me enlighten you to the truth regarding the tales and fables identified:

Noah's Flood: There was no flood that covered the earth, destroyed life on earth, except for Noah and his family. In fact, a number of civilizations in the Middle East used a flood story, but with different actors and mode of escape. Use your head, the Ark would be impossible to build. Oh, with God's help. Please.

Plagues in Egypt: In the past few years, the African country, Cameroon suffered the same scenarios as the alleged Egyptians at the charge by Moses. The truth in Cameroon and ancient Egypt was movement of the earth's plates which resulted in toxic gases rising from the underground. (Jerusalem is due an earthquake within the near future. The United States is not the only country in the world with earthquake faults).

Jews fleeing Egypt: The Arab Hebrew were a Nomadic people that would enter another country in search of food, water, etc., for their clan and animals. However, the Arab Hebrew did not want to blend in with the society. No! Their claim of being God's Chosen People led to the same turmoil in Egypt, as the United States is encountering today. Sure, most likely a number of Arab Hebrew departed Egypt seeking another Arab ethnic group to intimidate and or murder. (Egypt still has Arab Hebrews among their population). They allegedly found the Palestinian (Canaanites) to murder and take their land. Should sound familiar.

Oh, I almost forgot a greater scam by Arab Hebrews, which is Moses and the Ten Commandments. Individuals familiar with the Bible's version of the flight from Egypt and the infamous movie "Ten Commandments" should find the following interesting:

An expedition, by a noted U.S. movie producer, attempted to retrace the route taken by the Arab Hebrews out of Egypt. Of interest was the mount where Moses, allegedly, received the Ten Commandments from God. The team discovered an encampment and evidence of encampment described in the Bible on top of a mountain-not Mount Siani.

The movie version revealed God through his control of the elements carving the commandments into stone tablets. Based on scripture, it is my opinion, that Moses or whomever, chiseled the tablet themselves. Allegedly, when Moses or whomever, came down from the mountain with the tablets his face was so burned he had to wear a veil. It is my accusation that the burned face came from camp fires needed for heat and light to chisel the stones. No supreme entity was present.

Our Ministers, Sunday School teachers, and of course, family members stressed upon us parts of the Old Testament and the New Testament. Jesus Christ was the main character throughout my childhood. Overall, the county was Protestant, including Catholics, but I did not know any individuals whose religion was Judaism.

Our community has changed now with a large influx of those of Judaism from states north of Kentucky. By way of their money, our community has become corrupted to the point of setting aside the U.S. Constitution. For example: at South Laurel High School's 209 graduation speech, a senior addressed the assembly where he told of Jews fleeing Egypt. Religion has no more place in the schools than politics. Schools should be the arena where truth is spoken.

Growing up during the 1950's, Americans felt secure, both economically and physically. Our President was General Dwight David Eisenhower, with an appointed Presidential Cabinet of Americans not hyphenated Americans. The Congress of the United States emulated the guidelines set forth by the Constitution of the Unites States. Americans were in Washington. Our founders would have been satisfied.

Race relations in Laurel County, as I recall, were without incident. Black Americans went to Black Schools, and Whites to White Schools. I remember one time at London's Indoor Theater, I sat in the balcony, but later learned the theater was segregated. Black Americans were to sit in the balcony. I went back to the balcony whenever I wanted. As far as communication with Black Americans, my only contact was with a family that did plumbing work. (An Aunt hired the family to put in the plumbing in one of the houses she had built for sale). Going further, in my home, Mother welcomed anyone to share our food and hospitality. She was a true American.

Family life, most of my life, was without a father. Even before Mother and my Father were divorced, my Father frequently came home on weekends; however he had no association with me. (He worked in Norwood, Ohio). So, at eleven, Mom was both mother and father. But even without a father, relatives supported Mother, and I was able to attend 4-H Camp, join the Civil Air Patrol, and visit my Aunts in Michigan and Ohio. (While in Michigan, my Aunt took me to Canada, to my first Big Boy Restaurant, and to the beautiful Roman style movie theaters in Detroit).

Laurel County is a sportsman dream. Locals fish, hunt for small game, coon and fox hunt. The area now has elk, deer, black bears and turkeys. You can swim in the many local ponds and lakes. Our state park, Levi Jackson, is part of the Cumberland Trail used to settle Kentucky and travel west. Likewise, Laurel County was selected by the late movie star Burt Lancaster to film the movie "KENTUCKIANS." Of note, London is the county seat of government, and is the home of the Federal Government's Judicial System for Southeastern Kentucky.

As with any beautiful land of mountains, trees, waterways, etc., life threatening situations often arise. This was the case for a short periods in parts of Laurel County prone to flood. However, the flooding situation was short lived as the U.S. Corps of Engineers used their engineering skills to build dams and other projects that ended the flooding. Also, from the flooding projects came a marvel of the Eisenhower Administration - U.S. Interstate 75. (A highway beginning in Canada and ending in the state of Florida).

After years of being divorced, my Mother remarried. Needless to write, I was not happy. I was forced to move to a farm and change high schools. Almost two years passed and the situation between my Stepfather and me did not get any better. So, instead of creating friction between my Mother and Stepfather, I visited the Air Force Recruiter's Office, located in Corbin, Kentucky. I signed up!

Being only 17 years old, my Mom had to sign her consent. Within a short period of time I was on my way to the Military Entrance Processing Station, Louisville, KY. At the MEPS, we were given medical examinations, completed more official forms, and swore an oath. The oath is the same as all federal employees sign in, that we would defend the U.S. Constitution against all enemies both foreign and domestic.

We departed Louisville late in the afternoon, aboard a Braniff Airline DC-3 (C-47), en-route to San Antonio, Texas. From the San Antonio International Airport, we traveled by bus to Lackland Air Force Base, San Antonio, Texas for basic military training. It was at Lackland where I began learning a vocation, which lasted for the next 20 years.

Lackland Air Force Base, Texas

As we disembarked form the Braniff Airlines fight from Louisville, Kentucky to San Antonio International Airport, Texas, we collected our thoughts about the days events. For myself, the Braniff flight was my first on a commercial aircraft. I had ridden on a U.S. Army helicopter relief flight once during a seasonal flood. The pilots took us school kids on a short flight. Equally impressive, arrival in Texas was the first time out West, and the first where English was a second language for some..

Here we were, a group of U.S. Air Force enlistees from the Commonwealth of Kentucky, walking toward the waiting Air Force enlisted personnel, standing patiently for our arrival. We were welcomed, our personnel folders turned over to the instructors, and asked to get on the blur air force base for the ride to Lackland Air Force Base, Texas. (Traveling to and from the airport is the closest our flight ever got seeing the city of San Antonio, Texas).

Going through the gates at Lackland, we saw the Air Policeman give permission for our bus to continue on base. The next stop was the barracks, that we would occupy for the next six to eight weeks. We were assigned rooms with two roommates and shown the community lavatory, the entire flight would have to share. (First example of the difference in living standards between the Marines and U.S. Air Force. No open bay barracks or steel hut). Following room assignments and general instructions, our peace and tranquility diminished. We were in the military now, so we endured fire drills throughout the night.

The next day began our six to eight weeks (Don't remember the exact number of weeks) of learning the Air Force's way of accomplishing daily tasks, and educated to the needs of the Air Force. We had our hair cut, went through a clothing line, visited the Base Exchange (like Wal-mart) to purchase hygienic products, shoe polish, etc., taught how to mend our clothing and sew on patches, stripes, etc. (Stripes, patches, etc., had to be in the exact designated areas or you would receive demerits).

Another example that we were in the military came either the first or second day. The flight had to pack up all their non-military clothing, or anything else the instructors did not want one to keep, and mail it to our home of record. For most of us, home of record was with our parents.

We were taught how to march, stand at attention, salute, and all the other military acts we felt at the time were a joke. (Over one's career, you learned the training served a valuable purpose). I recall one day while marching, the instructor halted the flight. The instructor asked that I came forward. Once I got into the proper position, he informed me and the flight that I was the only one that was in proper military step. I returned to my position and the flight proceeded to their destination.

In the 1960's, the U.S. Air Force's shoulder fired weapon of choice was the M-1 Carbine. The weapon could be fired either automatic or semi-automatic. We were taught how to breakdown, reassemble, and fire the Carbine.

Due to a severe hot weather period, our flight was excused from the normal physical training. In place of the training, we sat under our barracks practicing breaking down and reassembling the Carbine.

Although, we did not do a lot of physical training, I departed basic training, taller and 30 pounds heavier. At enlistment, I weighed 115 pounds soaking wet with two pounds of bananas. I returned to London, weighing 145 pounds.

Of course, we visited the gas chamber that is frequently shown in military movies where scenes of basic training are shown. Nothing to it. What was worse occurred later in my career when you had to put on the protective body suit during exercises. The suit, especially the head gear, was restrictive but you wore it, as it could save your life.

Besides the suit, the self application kits for nerve gas and other toxic substances was interesting. One in particular was the Pentagon shaped metal needle you would stab in a large muscle and then stick it through your clothing and bend the needle. The bent needle would show medics that you had already administered the shot as you would most likely be unconscious. The scariest part of basic training to me was the hours we spent in our seats being taught how we were subject to court martial for violating any of the provisions of the Uniform Code of Military Justice. (More codes to adhere than public laws).

Class studies: we were afforded class room study and lectures ranging from personal hygiene, first aid, sexual diseases and other subjects one would not have received in a non-military environment. My wish today regarding sexual awareness is that the military would have taught us, especially individuals like myself from the Bible Belt, a truthful history of the dangers of sexual intercourse, and how non-concern for the woman could lead to an un-wanted child or a shot-gun wedding. Another equally important subject, both in basic training and at your permanent duty station was PRIDE. To me, this five letter word and acronym instilled in us the importance of comradeship, personal appearance, integrity, racial/social equality and to respect the freedoms and rights we have as Americans.

Our technical instructors (TI) were not like the alleged Army or Marine Corps drill instructors the public hear so much about for their frequently cruelty to trainees. Without a doubt, had I been an Army or

Marine recruit, I would have surely washed out. For example, Air Force Instructors cannot put their hands on your person, nor use profanity against you. Of the trainers I trained under, they were individuals of integrity and high morals. A benefit to the United States Air Force.

Toward the end of our basic training, we learned the reason for a number of the administrative test we had taken. They were for our benefit as well as the Air Force. The test re-affirmed and/or strengthened our aptitude scores that would, allegedly, determine which Air Force Vocations one would be assigned following basic training. I had passed all the fields, but was strongest in the administrative field. However, in my case and a number of other airmen, the manpower needs of the United States Air Force's Strategic Air Command had priority over our scores. Some of my flight mates went to civil engineering (fire department, paint shop, road repair, etc.), food service, transportation and Law Enforcement and Security.

The interim vacation I was charged and air base assigned was to be at the 19th Combat defense Squadron, Strategic Air Command, homestead Air Force Base, Florida. At this assignment, I would be working much like a city policeman in the law enforcement branch of the vocation, a security person to guard the nuclear armed alert aircraft and secure the air base from unauthorized, outside forces.

The weeks at Lackland were not all spent in training. After a short period, we were given on-base liberty. This status allowed us to enjoy the many sporting activities, movies, Base Exchange Facilities, etc. as base personnel. Other squadrons received off-base passes, but our squadron was prone to be rejected for minor infractions. No San Antonio or Mexico.

Probably, one of the most lasting benefits from basic training was the association with Americans from all races, religions, and ethnic groups from across the fifty states and one U.S. Territory. We were all one organization and united as one air force and one people.

Our comradeship came in to play en-route to Atlanta International Airport. At Atlanta, those of us residing east of the Mississippi would change air carriers for their flight to the airport serving their hometown. Unfortunately, due to bad weather at Atlanta, our flight had the misfortune of stopping at an Alabama Airport. (Atlanta was closed due to fog and we had to make the stop until Atlanta opened). As we sat down in the air terminal restaurant, the waitress told us that she could not serve the black member of our group. We all told the waitress if she couldn't serve our friend, she couldn't serve any of us. An older lady came over and took orders from all of us. Regrettably, this was my first encounter with RACISM.

Homestead Air Force Base, Florida

At the Atlanta Airport, I changed to an airline that served my hometown of London, Kentucky. The carrier was Piedmont Airlines. The flight from Atlanta to London was approximately one hour. Upon arrival, my Mother and Sisters were waiting for me. After greetings and kisses, we loaded into Mom's automobile and headed to the farm. Since I was on a delay en-route to my first assignment, my number of days at home were limited. I paraded around the neighborhood in my uniform to show my girlfriend, friends, and former classmates, that the nerd had become an Airman Third Class in the United States Air Force. Toward the end of my leave, I told my Mother what personal items I no longer needed (including my automobile), so she could sell them.

My Mom and Sister drove me to the Greyhound Bus Station, in Corbin, Kentucky, to transport me to my first United States Air Force duty station, Homestead Air Base, Homestead, Florida (30 miles South of Miami). I still remember my Mother crying, that I was leaving for good at 17 years old.

Wow! The best bus ride I ever had in my lifetime. Naturally, wearing my uniform, I met this older girl, that got on the bus at one of the first stops in Tennessee. She was a musician going to a job in one of the major Tennessee cities. To this date, I wish I could remember her name, so that I could contact her. I definitely made it past second base.

Arrival in Miami, with a real life experience behind me, I took a taxi to a downtown hotel to spend the night. I would travel to the air base the following day. After settling down and changing clothes, with my testosterone high, I wanted to experience city life, that I had heard so much about. A Nudist Show down from the hotel. Sorry, too young. The club doorman would not allow me to enter.

The following morning, I asked a taxi driver to take me to Homestead Air Force Base. Departing the hotel, we drove through the first major city that I had ever visited by myself. Miami, 1960, was out of this world to a 17 year old.

The drive made his way to U.S. 1, and we headed South toward Key West, Florida. As the miles went by and we were approaching my destination, one could see the acres of farmland that feeds a large part of our population. Turning left off of U.S. 1, we approached the West Gate to the Air Base.

The Law Enforcement person (Air Policeman) approached the taxi driver and asked him to state his business. The driver motioned to me, whereas, I showed him my assignment orders and asked directions to the 19th Combat Defense Squadron Barracks. (Wow! What a beautiful air base).

The driver was paid and I entered the barracks to sign in with the Charge of Quarters (CQ). The CQ assigned me a room, and issued bedding, to which I retired to a new home and wonderful life.

A few days after signing in at base personnel, I learned first hand what former service members had told me about unusual projects an airman could encounter. I learned fast. The Division Commander wanted the base recreation department to build a golf course at ground site on base, that had to be cleared of debris before construction could begin. So myself, and a large number of new arrivals were trucked out to this rocky, grass spotted large field. Our job was to pick-up the rocks and other obstacles, and throw them into dump trucks. A beautiful golf course materialized from our labor.

The name of my squadron, 19th Combat Defense Squadron, surprised me. Not knowing the history of the Air Force, I never envisioned the Air Force would use the term "combat" as part of an organization of Air Force Personnel. The term combat, I related to the Army of Marine Corps.

Within a short time of my arrival, additional personnel were assigned, bringing the total number of new assignees to approximately 60. Naturally, being at the bottom of the totem pole, the enlisted member did not know of the events occurring in Southeast Asia, but apparently General Curtis LeMay did. War was coming.

Following normal base in-processing we learned of the Strategic Air Commands project called Tough Tigers. The 60 arrivals, which included me, would receive combat training to equal that of the U.S. Army.

Prior to starting our combat training, we learned our Air Force Instructors had attended an Army Combat Training School to prepare them for our training. Our training lasted approximately six weeks, and I suppose it emulated the real Army. Each day, we would have to stand formation and march in formation to and from the different training sites.

The base had built a combat obstacle course with all the events/obstacles one can see when watching a movie that shows Army personnel in combat training. We learned how to assemble/disassemble different weapons, had to qualify as a sharpshooter with a pistol, and shoulder fired weapon, plus hand-to-hand combat fighting with the base Judo instructor.

The obstacle training was not without humor and embarrassment. For myself, while running log obstacles that are placed at different heights (being a cocky young seventeen old), my foot caught on a log and I fell hurting my testicles, but I got up , shook it off, and continued.

A physically large friend from Georgia, was charged with being the Browning Automatic Rifle person. When it came time to hand-walk a ladder type obstacle over a flooded canal, he would go out part of the way, and become afraid or uncertain and have to return to solid ground. The instructor became irritated and threw the BAR into the canal, forcing my friend to recover the rifle from the water. I don't remember if he actually completed the hand-walk over the canal.

Having not been in face to face combat with the enemy, in Indo-China, or attacked while on a real-time patrol, I believe, our day and night combat assaults were probably as close as one could come to actual combat (I had to attend two separate like courses prior to my assignment in Southeast Asia and Indo-China; whereas, Florida was more realistic than the other two). For example, on one night assault, we (flight) had to lie in Florida swamp water, and mud until our supposed artillery support was completed. Following the artillery support, we began to move down the side of a canal when the opposing enemy force opened light and heavy weapons fire, and allegedly, mortar rounds. We dove for cover and returned their fire.

A day time assault, not far from base housing, had to be cancelled because of the alleged profanity, the flight was using against the opposing force. From graduation day forward, we were known as "The Strategic Air Command's Tough Tigers."

Later in my career, I learned one of my comrades from the 19th Defense Squadron was killed in South Vietnam.

In late 1959, a Cuban Doctor (Fidel Castro), his Brother (Raul Castro), and a Communist friend (Che' Guevara) forced Cuban President Batista to resign and flee Cuba. The Eisenhower Administration's Central Intelligence Agency devised a war plan to forcefully re-take Cuba from the newly declared Communist Government of Cuba. But wait, a new American President had been elected in November 1960. The new President, John F. Kennedy, and Kennedy's Brother, Bobby Kennedy, denied U.S. and mercenary military support to the free Cubans attempting to overthrow Castro's Government (Regardless of what the news pundits say, the Cuban failure was not fault of the Central Intelligence Agency. Place the failure where the buck stopped - John F. Kennedy and Bobby Kennedy).

After the Bay of Pigs Incident (Cuban Invasion), Cuba became a greater thorn to President Kennedy. The period of August - November 1962 became known as the Cuban Missile Crisis. The Soviet Union wanted to build missile sites in Cuba capable of striking the United States. To this find, President Kennedy ordered a U.S. Naval Blockade of Cuba that resulted in our air base being turned into an armed Army and Marine Corps staging area. The beauty and peaceful life of the Air Base was broken by the hundreds of tents, and was equipment staged/parked on the Division Commander's grass.

The Department of Defense assigned a Tactical Air Command (TAC) Fighter Wing at the airbase. However, instead of establishing a separate security function, the TAC Wing's Security Personnel (Air Police) were integrated into the 19th Combat Defense Forces. Based on the combined actions of TAC and SAC units, the fighter wing was presented, in person, by President Kennedy, the Presidential Unit Award. As a member of the squadron, the 19th Combat Defense Squadron received the unit award.

As one of the many guards securing the roadways, I saw President Kennedy drive by with the vehicle's top down. He looked really tired, naturally so.

Extremely important to the Kennedy legacy, the United States was deeply involved in a secret war in the Kingdom of Laos and supporting the French Government against the Viet Cong and North Vietnam.

Kennedy was in over his head, and thereby, upset a number of revengeful individuals.

As heavily taxed as President Kennedy was with the Cuban Crisis, the status of the imprisoned free Cuban's repatriation to the United States remained outstanding. Once again, United States Air Force Personnel came to resolve the situation in the form of a U.S. Air Force Reserve Lieutenant Colonel.

The reason I know this fact, is because, whenever the Lieutenant Colonel would be scheduled to arrive at the Air Base to fly to Cuba for talks with the Cuban Government, I would be pulled from whatever post I was assigned, to work the Air Base's West Gate (This was the gate Lt. Colonel would arrive). A resolution was finally reached.

At the release of the Bay of Pigs (Cubans from Cuban jails), our Air Base was the reception and processing center for the returnees. The on-base site was at the Black Hangar, located on the airport apron. Here the returnees were greeted as heroes, met their families, were provided clothing, and given money, prior to their busing to Miami Beach for a gallant party in their honor. Also, many of the returnees became members of the United States Army. On the negative side, allegedly, Castro said, "They were cowards," and made all of them wear a yellow shirt at release.

Of interest, during the Cuban Crisis, day to day normal law enforcement and security tasks, had to be accomplished. Whereas, we worked 12 hour shifts, and on special occasions pulled additional duty at night. On one heartbreaking evening, I was dispatched to a Leisure City Bar to investigate an incident involving an Air Force Technical Sergeant (Leisure City was a subdivision of homes outside the West Gate of the Air Base). After I arrived at the scene, I went inside the bar. Dade County Police Officers had already removed the bodies of the victim and the Technical Sergeant (TSGT).

What I learned was the TSGT and the victim were allegedly, boyfriend and girlfriend. The Sergeant had visited the bar and the two became engaged in a verbal dispute. The Sergeant departed, but returned with a pistol. He walked behind the bar and shot his girlfriend and then himself. Prior to my return to the Air Base, an Office of Special Investigation Officer arrived. We both submitted reports. I was 19 years old.

Homestead Air Base was a city within itself. The Base Commander was the Mayor, with the military personnel to maintain both military and on-base housing for dependents. Likewise, any domestic criminal activity or hospital treated injury was investigated by the Air Police.

Regarding hospital treated injuries, one evening I was dispatched to the base hospital to record the injury of an Army trooper who was on leave in South Florida. Findings revealed the trooper walked into a bar in Perrine, Florida (low income area, known for domestic and personal violence), and was attacked by an unknown aggressor. He was severely cut, and had lost a lot of blood. Dade County Police Officers assumed responsibility of the investigation, being the assault occurred in Dade County. I made my report and returned to patrol.

Before, I identified that our base was saturated with Army and Marine personnel, for which their presence posed a problem for law enforcement. For example, dependents in base housing were reporting peeping toms. So a few of us worked additional hours on patrol in attempt to capture the person or persons. I was lucky, I caught an unauthorized soldier walking inside base housing, without a need or right to be there. I apprehended the soldier, and turned him over to the desk Sergeant. I do not know the outcome of his case.

Hazardous Duty: My big mouth and opinions probably was the reason I was assigned to a hazardous material site for a couple of days. The site was not normally manned unless the site held canned (50 gallon drums) hazardous material. The drums would not remain long at the site until sent elsewhere. Where I don't know.

Due to the massive security problem the Cuban Crisis posed, on a number of occasions, I was assigned to patrol the outer perimeter of the Air Base between Crash Gate 1 and Crash Gate 2. The area was typical Florida swamp land with water canals, scrub pine trees, and other foliage that was home for alligators, poisonous snakes, and dangerous four legged animals. As far as human danger, outside Crash Gate 2 was a migrant labor camp which housed both Spanish speaking legal and illegal persons. What made the human element questionable, was near the area where cocked B-52 aircraft were on alert.

Over the period of alert, I had never encountered anything or anyone, out of the ordinary during my tour of duty. The day started out the same, I became bored, but found some parachute cord in the foliage. I made a bow using the string, and cut some limbs for arrows. DUMB. During my walks between the gates, I had observed one particular lazy alligator swimming in one of the canals. I walked to his location, and began shooting the arrows at him. Finally, he became angry, and started to climb out of the water (Yes, I had weapons, but if I shot the gator, I would probably be in jail or dishonorably discharged. I went on my way and left the gator to do gator things).

Returning to the real world, the morning of the migrant incident, we were briefed, that should we apprehend anyone, to turn off our hand held radios, once our message was acknowledged, in order to conserve the batteries.

While returning to Crash Gate 1 from Crash Gate 2, I observed a black male walking toward the B-52 area. I challenged him. I contacted Central Security Control that I had apprehended an individual and after acknowledgement, I turned off the radio. Within a very short time, two strike teams (similar to SWAT) screeched to a stop at my position. The male was placed in the truck for interrogation at the command center. I later learned the individual was pretty shocked by his treatment. I'm sure I would have been due to world events at the time.

Addressing the cocked B-52's. I often wondered about our exposure (guarding the aircraft) to health damaging radiation or other dangerous emissions from maintenance personnel working on the aircraft's radar and radar controlled guns. Even more troublesome, were the nuclear weapons aboard the aircraft. We were often within 10-15 feet of the weapons. Who knows?

Not every day was a duty day, so one evening a group of us were standing in the parking lot outside our barracks, when a fellow airman drove up. He told us he knew of a hideaway bar in the everglades down U.S. 1. We jumped into two automobiles and headed South. We located the well illuminated building displaying beer signs, and other alcohol advertisements. After parking, we walked through the front door of the establishment, and sat at the bar. A young woman came out , and asked if she could help us. I told her I wanted a Tequila drink. She replied, "Sir, this is not a bar, it is our home." She then asked us if we wanted a drink, but we refused, apologized, and departed back to the base.

December 31, 1962, I was working swing shifts (3:00 p.m. to 11:00 p.m.) and stood guard mount. As was the policy, the shift commander, on occasion, would select the best dressed airman, and give him or her the night off. December 31st was my night.

Later in the evening, I departed base to a private home in Homestead or Florida City (they connect), where there was a New Year's Eve Party. I knew of the non-adult party because as a gate guard, and on occasions, the visitor control person I knew of the party giver, and also, she was a friend of Bill Wilson, the son of an Air Force Sergeant residing on base. Bill was s student at the Virginia Military Institute and I knew him well enough to be welcome at the party.

Since 1963, I have been seeking information on what actually happened on the evening of December 31, 1962. Luck was with me, as I recently received copies of my military records, plus medical from the Department of Veteran Affairs. Naturally, I looked up the hospital report.

I had understood the accident was after January 1, 1963. It was not. According to hospital admission, the time was approximately 2200 hours, the night of December 31, 1962.

I had no idea of what caused the accident or what occurred. The report read that I failed to make a proper turn. Now everything makes sense.

After I was released the first time from the air force hospital. I visited the accident site. There were no stop sign or sign advising a forthcoming intersection, the road was not lighted but on the other side of the loading platform/building, the street continued with street lights. The road ended in a t-formation. Straight ahead was a set of railroad tracks and to the right and left were streets. I failed to make a turn as the hospital report reads. I saw signs on the pavement that I had applied the brakes once when I recognized the road was ending. The practice of fastening my seat belt, saved my life at the site. The outstanding Air Force Doctors put me back together.

Their were no charges against me by the county, city, state or the U.S. Air Force. Allegedly, my accident cost the squadron the prized leather chair, with the SAC emblem. The squadron with the least number of demerits won the chair. I guess I was responsible for a large number of demerits.

Reading further in the hospital report, I learned I was in and out of a coma for an extended period of time. There were lacerations to my body and kidney damage. After approximately 12 days, I was released to full duty as an Air Policeman. Immediately, I began to have terrible headaches, back pain and a short temper. I returned to the hospital where X-Rays were taken that revealed damage to my lower spine. I was hospitalized for bed rest and then fitted for a back brace. I was released from the hospital with a brace for six months from atop my buttocks to my shoulder.

For approximately one year before and after the Cuban Crisis, I was associating with a girl that resided with her Staff Sergeant brother on base housing. After some months of dating and meetings, I told her that I didn't want any more contact with her. Bad mistake.

Shortly after the breakup call, I received a telephone call from her closest friend telling me that my friend was going to kill herself. Like a fool, I called her back. The encounters became more personal with sexual intercourse at her brother's home, in her mother's vehicles on the beach, etc. Alas, she told me she was pregnant. I asked her to marry.

At the wedding in the base chapel, my close friend told me not to marry. I responded that I had to because my mother would be extremely upset. After we married, I learned she was not pregnant, but naturally, she soon was with child.

My mother gave me the money to put a down payment on a home north of the air base. Mom and family members sent us pots, pans, linen, etc. to set up house. The wedding was in April, but I soon received transfer orders to the Republic of South Korea. So much for marriage.

Kunsan Air Base

Shot gun weddings do not work! The worst part is, there is usually a child or children from this type of wedding. It is the children that are hurt. When one divorces, either the wife or the husband, becomes the villain. In my divorce, I was the bad person. However I was fortunate, as over the years my daughter realized that her Mother played an important part in the divorce.

As previously identified, I received orders for re-assignment to Kunsan Air Base, Republic of Korea (South Korea), shortly after the wedding. Three of my squadron members received the same assignment. Two of the three were friends, the other an adversary. We all arrived at Homestead at approximately the same time, and were graduates of the Tough Tiger Training course.

One friend was like a brother (his children called me Uncle). He had a part time job driving new cars from the Miami Dock to Homestead, Florida car dealers (he always had some type of part time job). I suppose the knowledge of you drive automobiles came from one of his jobs, and/or associates. The idea was for the three of us to drive a California registered vehicle from the Miami-Dade area to California. The only money involved for us would be for gas and maintenance, if needed. We would have complete freedom, no airline or Greyhound bus. The idea did not wash with my wife, so my two friends and I boarded a Greyhound bus in Homestead for the long journey to Fairfield, California (Fairfield is the city outside the Travis Air Force Base Military Reservation).

My wife was pregnant, but her Mother lived with us in the home we purchased after a month or so of being married. My wife would be able to share her Mother's car so she could receive health care at the Homestead Air Force Base Hospital, utilize the Commissary, Base Exchange facilities, and remain with her friends from high school. My Air Force pay, through allotments, would pay the mortgage, plus provide my wife's living expenses. My Mother-in-Law worked, so there should not have been any problems financially.

We arrived at Fairfield, a day before we were scheduled to report to the Military Airlift Terminal at the air base. We checked in at a hotel. Two beds and a cot. My friends decided to go out for the evening, but I remained in the hotel room. Soon after my friends departed, the telephone rang. It was my wife checking up on me. She had called different hotels in Fairfield until she found which one I was staying in.

The next morning, the three of us took a taxi to Travis, and the passenger terminal. For information sake, a military terminal is no different from a civilian airport terminal, other than the military boarding sequence. We checked in at the passenger counter with our Permanent Change of Station (PCS) Orders in our hand, checked our baggage, and received our boarding passes. Since there is no First, Business, or Economy Class, we waited in the terminal until the first letter of the last name of each traveler was called (W for Wilson was near the last person called). The aircraft's seating configuration was tight, knees hitting the seat in front of you.

Once airborne, we departed the bickering and name calling of a disgruntled wife. Turned out to be a wish, not reality.

The flight was extremely long. I don't remember if we stopped in Guam for refueling, but I do remember the refueling stop at Tokyo's International Airport.

The flight from Tokyo to Seoul, Republic of Korea (Kimpo Air Base) wasn't too long. At touchdown, we made our way through military customs, and entered the main terminal building. What we saw and smelled, were scenes and smells unknown to us young Airmen.

The terminal was bustling with women, some with tears, and others with big smiles. Each lady and the environment emitted a strange odor which turned out to be Kiamichi, a fermented cabbage meal (a common staple in Korea).

From the airport/military terminal, we were transported to the transient barracks, for our en-route stay at Kimpo (Seoul). The purpose of the delay was to in-process in country.

My two friends and the adversary decided to go to the local village to become acquainted with the alcohol and women (One could only drink OB beer and not eat any local food. The Koreans used human feces as fertilizer). I remained on base, in the barracks.

I don't remember how, but I learned a person that I went to school with at Hazel Green High School (and also the husband of my farm girlfriend), was stationed at the air base. He was a pharmacy technician (He wasn't subjected to the needs of the Air Force at vocational assignment).

I went for a visit (as maybe it was my Mother that told me about my fellow Kentuckian), to make an appearance, and ask questions as to what to expect from the assignment. He said the airport scene was normal, as ladies were saying goodbye to their boyfriends, and lining up new ones for the next 13 months. He stated that he did not associate with the Korean women at the base or nearby village/town, but he did have a girlfriend in Seoul (There was an extremely large American presence in Seoul, and it's immediate surroundings). He confirmed the smell was Kiamichi.

Following in-country processing, those of us that had to lay over in Kimpo were cleared to proceed to our assignment - Kunsan Air Base, a major USAF Air Base in the Republic of Korea. I do not know if the ROK are co-assigned).

The USAF had cocked F-100 aircraft on alert, and the ROK had F-86 aircraft (Korean War vintage). Other USAF aircraft were the base C-47 and a L-20 (Beaver) aircraft with dual purposes. The C-47 was used to occasionally pickup mail at Kimpo, and fly missions dictated by higher headquarters. The L-20 aircraft had a similar mission, but as was the C-47, allowed rated pilots to receive their flight pay since they were not assigned to an F-100 Combat Billet.

Well to our surprise, the in-country/base processing was not over. We had to process in as airman assigned to Kunsan, were assigned barracks, issued ration cards, obtain driver's license, and be briefed on do's and don'ts in Korea. A greater surprise was the issuance of a Carbine, two loaded magazines, a pup-tent, and a medical kit (Issuance of the medical kit containing the pentagon shaped needle, cream, and the other medical items needed for chemical and/or bacteriological are a real attention getter. We were in the real world now, not basic training). Oh, one must not forget the gas mask which we had to maintain with periodic evaluations. Today, the North Koreans have denounced the Armistice that ended open hostilities between North Korea and the United States. There was an active Armistice during my tour.

For those of us assigned to the Combat Defense Squadron, our quarters turned out to be World War II Quanset Huts. The open bay hut was heated by a coal burning stove. The community bathroom was another Quanset hut yards away from the residential hut. Korea has some cold, snowy winters. We paid a Korean house person to keep the fires going.

Due to my physical profile (fractured lower spine), I was assigned to the Security Police's Armory. My duties were to hand out handguns and shoulder fired weapons with ammunition, at the beginning and end of each shift. The hours between shift change were spent cleaning weapons and maintaining the armory (I was still on my feet, and adding damage to my injured spine).

After a few months in the armory, I took the opportunity to seek a cross-train to a career field more in administration. Since my AQE (Aptitude) scores would permit me to cross-train into any Air Force vocation that did not require me to return to the United States to attend a technical school (As you may recall, the Law Enforcement and Security Career Field was assigned due to the needs of the Strategic Air Command).

Base personnel issued temporary orders for me to travel to Osan Air Base, ROK, which was the U.S. Air Force's Division Headquarters. At Osan, I met with the Officer In Charge of Division On The Job Training.

From the conversations with the training officer, review of manuals describing the tasks of each Air Force specialty, Aptitude scores, and my physical profile, I chose the Air Traffic Control Field (27X00).

The Air Traffic Control Field was multiple facet. One could be a 271X0 (Air Operations), which included Base Operations, the Command Post, Aircrew Scheduling, and Flight Records (I chose Base Operations). A progression of the 27X00 field provided for vocations, as an Air Traffic Control Tower, Ground Control Approach (GCA), Command & Control Center (Command Post), and Combat Controller. The Base Operations vocation allowed one to sit and stand in the accomplishment of their duties, plus there was no heavy lifting. I retired from the Air Operations Career Field as a 27199, Air Operations Superintendent.

The new career field opened a new and pleasant avenue for me. Since I was now assigned to the Combat Support Group Squadron, my quarters was a two-story wooden barracks with central air & heat, but still a community bath (one on each floor). One remembers being soaked with soap, and the water pressure would cease. You would have to wrap a towel around you and go to another barracks to finish your shower. I had one roommate who was the C-47's crew chief.

My new duty section was at a Joint Base Operations Facility. In this facility, we worked and trained with the South Korean Air Force, and spoke with the Korean en-route Air Routing Traffic Control Center and Flight Service Station (One day a voice on the direct line to the en-route center told me to go back to the United States. Believe me, I would have rather been in the States). The on-base Air Traffic Control Tower was manned by U.S. Air Force Controllers. The ROK Sergeant that I worked with was named, Sergeant Yu (Sergeant Yu had a black belt in karate). My two Air Force enlisted supervisors were, Staff Sergeant Spence and Staff Sergeant Wilson (No relation).

Since my roommate was Base Flight's C-47 Crew Chief, and my duties afforded the opportunity to be an additional aircrew member during my days off. In-country flights allowed me to observe the war ravaged country from a birds eye view, which was extremely different from ground level observation. In my mind, I could visualize the murder and hardships imposed on the Korean people by the North Koreans, Chinese, and in rare cases, the U.S. military.

Since I was learning my trade through On-The-Job Training, a flight to Itazuke Air Base, Japan, to utilize thus learning first hand International Civil Aviation Organization's (ICAO) policies and procedures (The ICAO is a branch of the United Nations that is responsible for the safe and secure management on International airspace, policies, and procedures for aircrews to enter foreign airspace and then land at their host countries airport and/or military air base. Airways and reporting points are just like Interstates, intersections, and traffic signs on the ground).

The flight was a unique experience, I not only planned the flight by utilizing ICAO en-route charts, approach booklets, both Secret and non-classified Foreign Clearance Guide. The en-route supplement provided us with the information we needed once we arrived at Itazuke.

The flight to Japan, not counting the flight planning experience, taught me to be more attentive. For example, as an Aircrew Member, I was authorized to use aircrew quarters, instead of going to the base transient facility. So, after checking into my room and changing into civilian clothes, I walked out of the base gate to the Japanese village (I had never been on the ground in Japan, plus, I wanted to see what my ex-brother-in-law had told me the truth about Japan. I was not impressed).

Early the next morning, I heard an unusually loud, piercing sound that I thought may have been the base's alert horn (Recently, the base movie at Kunsan, was interrupted, followed with the announcement that certain members of the Combat Defense Squadron must report to their unit. They were on their way to South Vietnam). I jumped out of bed, put my flight suit on, grabbed my bag and headed to the billet office to hail a military taxi. Before I made an ass out of myself, the horn went off again, and from my position, I learned the horn was from some type of large ship in the Fukuoka's Harbor (Fukuoka is a large shipping port in Japan). I had never heard a ship's horn before.

Returning from Itazuke, our approach to Kunsan's airfield was pleasant, with a secure feeling. One could see the on-going construction of a new electrical grid and sewage system to assume with creditability, U.S. presence at Kunsan would increase.

Amazing to me was the equipment the Korean's used in their construction work. Movement of large concrete electrical power poles were transported on hand-drawn carts. The Korean's had a device all on A-Frame, that is, the item fit on the frame, then the Koreans could carry the item. I never saw one piece of construction machinery used to dig the sewage ditches, etc. The Koreans used picks and shovels, and bamboo poles as ladders, wall containers, pilings, etc (Not paying attention, one evening when I was returning from dinner at the Airman's Club, I fell into one of the newly dug sewage ditches). The Koreans didn't mark their diggings by any method. They may place a board or log in order to walk over the opening, but no light or warning that the ditch was there.

More on construction. I learned an Air Policeman had apprehended a Korean being on the airbase too early. When interrogated, the Korean was a day laborer, with a shovel. He wanted to arrive early so he could have a better dirt site to load. He was paid by the number of loads departing the site.

Another case. An Air Policeman apprehended an individual attempting to sneak onto the grassy area surrounding the airfield, parking areas, etc. The individual wanted to cut the straw to build and/or repair his home. The Koreans mixed straw and mud, much like the early American Western Settlers to build their homes.

Now returning to my personal life. From the day I departed Florida, until the day I knew my marriage was over, I never once entertained going to town to be with another woman. The camel's back was broken when I didn't receive any mail from my Wife over an extended period of time, coupled with the fact, she gave up our beautiful home in Florida to move to Charleston, South Carolina. She moved in with her Aunt while her Mother returned to her husband in a small South Carolina town. Sounds vague, but there was more.

Having never been to any town in Korea, I decided to go and see what the Korean village looked like. My friend that had accompanied me from Homestead Air Force Base was one of the Air Policemen who was a Police Town Patrolman. Using his guidance, I traveled to Kunsan.

Kunsan was approximately thirteen miles from the air base. Transportation to and from the village/city was provided, at cost, by the Base Exchange's Taxi Service. To make the situation worse, Kunsan and parts of Korea had a curfew, which was imposed during certain hours. One reason (allegedly) for the curfew, may have been reports of sporadic gunfire, originating from one of the hamlets between the base and Kunsan. We were informed that some of the residents were Communist Sympathizers.

Finally arriving in Kunsan, I was disturbed by the self-imposed separation of the different races among U.S. military members. We learned Blacks and Whites frequented separate clubs, and with certain women. However, to my knowledge there was never any physical violence due to race.

I did have sexual intercourse with a couple of different Korean women in their homes. I stopped, when I learned that they were engaged to Airman at the airbase (I told my Wife when she asked).

After my first trip to town, I wrote my Mother about the travel and my observations. Since I was from the rural United States, our family's life was austere, however what I observed, made me realize what we had in the United States of America. En-route to town, one could see running water in canals and ditches. The streams were used for washing clothing, cleaning food, bathing, and on one occasion, I saw an indigenous person urinating in the stream.

Hamlet homes were made of straw and mud. We learned during the Winter months, Koreans would rip up the asphalt roadways for fuel. Speaking of fuel, most of the buildings and/or homes I visited were heated by bricks of charcoal under the structure's floor. Too often individuals were killed by the toxic fumes created by the charcoal.

One can understand why the American military man became partners with the Korean female. My friend had a Korean girlfriend, who gave birth to his son. He asked me to check on policies and procedures for marrying a Korean national. After I reported the findings, he gave up the idea.

I had a close, personal, no sexual involvement friend, that worked in the Airman's Club. Her name was Ms. Hae Cha Pae. Her Father was a Korean Dog Handler that worked for the Combat Defense Squadron.

It should be noted that during the thirteen months I spent in Korea, a great number of those days were spent consuming alcoholic beverages at the Airman's Club. Often when I walked into the club, Ms. Pae would ask me if I needed money for food or a haircut. If I needed the money, she would give me her money, and if she had no money, she would ask another airman in the club to buy her a chicken dinner. She would then give the money to me.

To show my appreciation, on one of my trips to Japan, I traveled to the harbor city of Fuokoya for a two fold purpose. One was to see a large Japanese city, and the other was to purchase Ms. Pae some personal items not available in Kunsan.

With Ms. Pae, I made an ass out of myself. I made things worse by getting upset when Ms. Pae was forced to marry a much older man picked by her Father. If I could, I would like to return to Kunsan and pay my respects to her. She was a beautiful friend.

In October 1965, our 13 months in Korea ended. My transfer orders came with my new assignment being Malsmstrom Air Force Base, Montana. Another SAC base. Homestead was SAC. I was going home to see my daughter, MeLissa Latrell Wilson, born on May 7, 1965. I had no idea of what would become of my marriage.

Montana

The last visit to Kimpo Air Base, Seoul, South Korea, was much different from 13 months earlier. We understood the people, the smells, memories of what we did and did not do. An educational tour both military and personal.

At the terminal, we checked in, awaited for our last name to be called and boarded Military Air Command's contracted civilian airliner for a flight to Travis Air Force Base, California. The aircraft refueled in Tokyo, Japan, then back into the wild blue yonder for the United States. When I write back to the U.S. that's what the airliner did. We flew direct from Tokyo to Travis Air Force Base. The pilot told us we had a tail wind from the jet stream. A long, long, long flight.

At Travis, we cleared U.S. Customs, made telephone calls to our families and loaded onto a Greyhound Bus for the San Francisco International Airport. At the airport by the bay, some boarded flights to Atlanta for transfer to their hometown airport or nearest major city's airport to their rural home. I was in the group that changed at Chicago O'Hara, the worlds busiest airport.

Touchdown at O'Hara. Once again to the telephone to inform my family that I had arrived in Chicago and I would be boarding an aircraft for the Columbia, Tennessee airport. Naturally, when I informed my wife of my estimated time of arrival in Tennessee, she would be there waiting with my baby daughter, MeLissa Latrell Wilson.

Interesting, I made a number of telephone calls and seemed to reach the same long distance operator each time. Over the period of time the operator and I spoke, we established an apparent rapport. In fact, she, the operator, suggested I stay in Chicago with her. I told her I had been away in South Korea for 13 months and I had a baby daughter I had never seen. (In hindsight, based on events in Tennessee, I should have stayed with her).

A pleasant non eventful flight and a pretty good landing by the pilot at the Columbia airport. Into the terminal I go, pick-up my luggage and head for the terminal area. No wife, no daughter. Several hours, I mean several hours passed, then my wife, daughter, and brother-in-law showed up in a brand new Ford automobile. I learned later that I had purchased the vehicle in some manner. (Never give anyone full Power of Attorney, I gave both wives a full Power of Attorney and the Golden Shaft was my reward). The very first words out my wife's mouth were "were you faithful to me?" No! I told her the truth. She then passed my child to me, (My wife told me on different occasions later that MeLissa was not my child. My daughter after she became a wife and mother said to me that anyone with eyes knew I was her father. This made me feel good),

Regarding my association with a Kunsan lady. That came after the months I described where I had no communications from my wife, and I strongly suspected her adultery. I visited Kunsan City.

I met an American woman named Rosie. We were together in her home a number of times, however I ended our relationship when I learned she was engaged to an Airman from Arkansas.

The time in Columbia was spent with my wife and her family in a Christian Community Home. (To this day, I don't know why all the other people were there, other than her family). While in Tennessee, my wife, daughter, and I visited the Grand Ole Opry and Graceland. (I had the opportunity to hold my screaming daughter in the Opry's lobby while my wife was entertained). As stated previously, she had purchased a new automobile and disposed of our South Florida home. To date, I still do not know what happened to our personal property.

Military leave was ending, so we packed up the Ford. My wife, daughter, and I began our journey to Great Falls, Montana: Home of Malmstrom Air Force Base.

The trip to Montana went well for our daughter, as always, my wife was never happy with anything. If I remember correctly, we stayed in the base's family transient housing until my wife located a home.

The residence we selected turned out to be a converted brick car garage. Our new home was located in a quiet, beautiful neighborhood in the city of Great Falls, Montana. The home was perfect for my small family.

Wow! The people in Great Falls and the Base Operations Facility that I would be working with were out of this world. Wonderful people. My duties would be in aircraft dispatch and flight publications. (The Non-Commissioned Officer in Charge of Base Operations and the Base Operations Officer had their act together), I learned so much regarding the requisition, distribution and management of aircrew flight publications from the NCOIC. I later improvised on his policies resulting in saving the command a lot of money.

Being a Strategic Air Command Base (the best command in the Air Force), Malmstrom did not have a lot of transient aircraft and no bomber aircraft assigned. The reason being was Malmstrom supported Intercontinental Ballistics Missiles (ICBM) sites scattered through the Montana Countryside. Our air traffic was mostly local helicopter flights supporting the missile silos and sites. Daily civilian contract flights kept the base support ground crews proficient, but the main attraction was the infrequent arrival and departure of the C-133 aircraft.

The C-133 and occasionally a special modified aircraft would deliver and/or take-out and ICBM. The Montana experience looked promising. A chance to excel and be with my family.

Promise soon ended. My wife changed her mind in our living quarters. The reason was, my wife brought her mother and nephew from Tennessee to live with us. (Her mother was a great person). Naturally with the increased bodies, the converted garage was not suffice.

The first area she wanted to move into was a questionable part of the city - crime, etc. - I said no. her next location was a World War II Row housing block. (Shot-gun houses consisting of three homes. A first time in seeing these type homes, but later during a trip to Sydney, Australia, the suburbs, were dominated by this type of home),

The World War II structures were sturdy with enough room for the five of us. On one side of our residence were two young women. The other side was occupied by a young, military couple. (Needless to say, the residence was not the environment for a jealous woman). Soon, the ranting began, according to my wife, I not only wanted to have sexual intercourse with the two single women, but also with my neighbor's wife.

The jealousy did not end with the neighboring women. Through fate, the moon, or whatever, my daughter was born on my young sister's birthday. Based on my sister's birth and undying love for my mother, our home was in constant turmoil. Could the situation get any worse? Yes! I learned there was an arrest warrant in South Carolina for me.

The warrant was because of the Ford automobile, which I wrote about previously. I learned my wife's step-father, Mr. Virgil Warren, had a different opinion as to who owned the automobile. So, here we go on emergency leave; to Hampton, South Carolina, in an attempt to resolve one of many situations she brought to bear. In Hampton, my wife's lawyer worked out a plan with Mr. Warren and the court. (I believe her lawyer was also her lover during my assignment in Korea). The plan entailed borrowing money from the Malmstrom Air Force Base Credit Union to pay for the automobile. I paid off the car while I was stationed in the Kingdom of Laos.

Returning to the Korean assignment for a period. As I revealed previously, I consumed a lot of alcohol during my 13 months in Korea. When I returned to the United States I stopped - cold turkey. Naturally, the termination of alcohol input to my body created an imbalance or whatever, within my body functions. Believing in God at the time, which meant for sure that I would split Hell wide open, I became a nuisance to a local Great Falls doctor. I do apologize to the doctor for my actions.

My assignment in base operations was going extremely well as I was learning a lot from the Master Sergeant in Charge of Base Operations. However, home time was terrible. To this end, one evening the telephone rang. The caller was my ex-crew chief roommate from Kunsan Air Base, Korea. He and his aircrew were remaining over-night at the air base and asked if I would meet him at a local restaurant/club.

Big mistake. The crew chief and I were eating at a table when in walked my wife. She created quite a scene for everyone's entertainment.

The relationship between my wife and I became worse. For example, one evening in her rage, she attempted to strike my head with a coke bottle. My daughter was in my arms.

I had had enough. I departed the residence and checked into a local motel. My wife called saying my mother was ill, so she could speak to me. In a short period of time, my wife, daughter and her family departed back to South Carolina and other parts of the country.

With the wife gone, I had car payments, child support, money for my estranged wife and rent to pay. Having a hard struggle, I invited an airman to share the apartment and rent with me. (Big mistake). Luck revealed her pretty head. I received orders for assignment to Don Muang Royal Thai Air Base, Kingdom of Thailand.

Interesting, from the time my wife departed, I never received any mail at my residence. However, I received a letter from my wife via one of the women next door. Years later, I learned my wife had written the Great Falls Post Office and had the mail, including mine, forwarded to her address.

My assignment to Base Operations and Great Falls will always have a place in my heart and mind. Had I been a sports person, I would have been in heaven. Equally important, the people of Great Falls were understanding and helpful in every way. I hope I still have friend in the city.

Bangkok, Kingdom Of Thailand

With my wife and daughter gone, I volunteered to duty in South Vietnam. My volunteering served two purposes: One, living expenses would be cheaper and I would receive extra money for being overseas. Second, I heard airman/soldiers could volunteer to be helicopter gunship gunners during their off duty period. I still don't know if the gunner story is true, as I didn't make it to South Vietnam.

At receipt of orders, I schedules a mover to transport our personal propertyto my wife's address. I departed Montana only with personal papers and clothing.

My first destination from Montana was Kentucky, to visit my mother and sisters. From Kentucky, I had an en-route temporary duty assignment at Hamilton Air Force Base, California. At Hamilton, we were given a refresher course in the use and maintenance of weapons we may have to use in Southeast Asia. From Hamilton, back to Travis Air Force for another Military Airlift Command's contract flight to Bangkok, Kingdom of Thailand.

The Bangkok flight was not direct and long like the Tokyo to Travis flight. We stopped in Hawaii and the island of Guam to refuel. Seating was the same, knees against the seat in front.

When we entered Thai Airspace, the cabin crew distributed customs and immigration forms. Once we started our approach to the Bangkok International Airport/Don Muang Royal Thai Air Base, I looked out the window to see what the terrain like was surrounding the dual use airport. The terrain reminded me of Homestead Air Force Base, Florida. You saw the identical water canals, marshes, sea-grass weed. I was back in Florida.

Before we start with our summary of the Bangkok, Thailand assignment, I will provide a brief history of U.S.- Thai Relationship:

"The official American military presence in Thailand started in April 1961 when an advanced party of the USAF 6020th Tactical (TAC) Group arrived at Don Muang at the request of the Royal Thai government to establish an aircraft warning system."

"Also, in April 1961, a small detachment of F-102 "Delta Daggers" from the 509th Fighter-Interceptor Squadron based a Clark AB Philippines, were sent to Don Muang under Operation Bell Tone. For the next several years, a minimum of four F-102 interceptors were kept on alert at Don Muang."

"Then in November 1961, four RF-101C, reconnaissance aircraft of the 45th Tactical Reconnaissance Squadron stationed a Misawa AB, Japan and their photo lab arrived at Don Muang."

On 15 May 1962, the Military Assistance Command was set up (MACT) at Don Muang.

In November 1962 the 2nd division assumed control of the 6010th TAC Group. In August the group was re-designated the 35th Tactical Fighter Group. The 35th TAC Group consisted of the following units:

- 35th Air Base Squadron - located at Don Muang
- 331st Air Base Squadron - located at Takhli RTAFB
- 332nd Air Base Squadron - located at Ubon RTAFB
- Det # 1, 35th Tactical Group - located at Korat RTAFB"

"By mid -1964 the situation in Southeast Asia was ambiguous. North Vietnam was determined to take over South Vietnam. Communist rebel forces were making military and political gains in Laos. The United States was taking over the role of "protector" from France in the area and the fear that Communism would prevail over the democratic governments in the region."

On 31 July 1964, based on a false charge against the North Vietnamese, President Lyndon B. Johnson ordered more forces to support the west-allied South Vietnam government and additional USAF forces were dispatched to Thailand.

In July 1965 the 25th TAC Group was re-designated 6236th Combat Support Group and again in April 1966 it was re-designated the 631 Combat Support Group. In March 1965 there were 1342 enlisted men stationed at Don Muang RTAFB, with their primary mission to provide support to all USAF units and detachments assigned to the base or other bases in Thailand.

Units assigned to Don Muang RTAFB were the following:

- 631st Combat Support Group - 2 C-47s
- Det # 4 315 Air Division - 7 C-1303s
- 509th Fighter Interceptor Squadron- 5 F-012s
- 452nd Air Refueling Squadron - 4 KC-135s"

One F-102 of the 509th FIS was lost to an air-to-air fired my a MIG-21 while flying a CAP (Combat Air Patrol) over Route Package IV on February 3, 1968.

Since Thailand was supposed to be neutral during the Vietnam War, the presence of the KC-135 at Don Muang was an embarrassment to the Thai Government. In response, the USAF expanded the Thai Navy Base at U-Tapao, Thailand to handle the KC-135s.

"The opening of U-Tapao also allowed the United States to route most of the logistics requirements in Thailand to be routed through that facility rather than having large cargo aircraft at the Thai Capital."

By 1970 most USAF operations had moved out of Don Muang, however, administrative personnel coordinating activities along with Military Assistance Command, Thailand (MACT) staff were assigned to the base until 1975."

Note: While I was assigned to Don Muang, the MACTHAI Command had a large fleet of transport aircraft used to fly logistics missions to South Vietnam. The U.S. Navy has a few sensitive mission A-3s.

I arrived at Don Muang in September 1966.

We disembarked from the aircraft and entered the Joint USAF/Thai passenger service and customs area. (Another new environment for the Kentucky boy). The Thai people were different from the South Koreans. They were extremely friendly and their dress was either western or Thai traditional. There was no smell of food products and no women saying good-bye to boy friends and seeking out new blood.

After clearing Thai/Military customs, all personnel were loaded on Thai buses for transport to our quarters at the Trocadero Hotel. The hotel was in an older part of Bangkok near the Chayo Phao River and the internationally famous Oriental Hotel. The hotel would be our home until such time an air force housing area and support facilities could be built near Don Muang and/or assigned to another contracted billet.

We were assigned two airman to a room. Later we met a Thai family that did the laundry for Americans at the hotel. (Our clothing, especially our white underclothes always smelled like oil or some other chemical or fluid). The spouse of the lady and father of the children was a Thai Air Force Officer at Don Muang.

The next few days, we would rife the Thai buses, belching black smoke with a strong odor, to and from the hotel to the militart side of the airport (Don Muang). At personnel, we were issued ration cards (used for buying cigarettes and Whiskey/Beer and certain restricted items), told of our duty assignments and informed of certain Thai customs we should avoid.

To my great surprise, I was to work in the Bangkok International Control Tower with both American and Thai Airman. (Outstanding rapport was established which helped me to learn Thai numbers and the Thai spoken language well enough to travel throughout the country and, later, in Laos by myself). My supervisor was Master Sergeant Whitby. My roommate was Technical Sergeant Larry Stith.

To accomplish administrative requirements, military pay questions, sick call, etc., we would ride the Air Force contracted bus to the military side of the international airport. Most American military structures were built. However, the base operations building was not ready for occupancy. Many of the areas on the military side retained ground water which was the home of malaria carrying insects, really poisonous snakes, and other animal life not normally found on a U.S. Military installation. The Thai family that did our laundry lived on the military installation near the base operations facility and joint Thai/U.S. Aircraft Parking Aprons. So, on the days that I didn't have to go to the military side, I would catch Thai Bus # 29 to the international airport.

After disembarking from the bus, I would usually go inside the terminal and mingle with the hundreds of tourist visiting Thailand. After maybe a sandwich or sweet roll in the terminal snack bar, I would take the elevator up to operations. All U.S. Air Crews had to file their flight plans with us in the control tower.

While working in the control tower, President Lyndon Baines Johnson and Lady Bird Johnson visited Thailand. The President and Mrs. Johnson visited South Vietnam prior to coming to Thailand. I was on duty the day the President and First Lady arrived, in operations.

In anticipation of Air Force 1's arrival, a base newspaper reporter was in operations to cover his arrival and take photographs. The base newspaper, KLONG NEWS, ran a column titled "CLEAR TO LAND". the photo showed Master Sergeant Warren F. Whitby and myself, Staff Sergeant Billy Ray Wilson, at the air traffic console.

Not long after the visit by President Johnson, the base operations facility was completed and we moved into the base operations building. With the change of duty location, base housing re-assigned me to an up-to-date modern western style apartment building. The building was owned by an active duty Thai General. Likewise, the building was not far from the capitol hotel which was the in-country classified headquarters for Project 404.

The general and I became friends, plus the Thai employees maintaining the clean snack bar were extremely friendly and would assist in anyway they could. In fact, the snack bar would allow you to run a monthly food and beverage tab. You paid at the end of the month.

If you believe in fate, the Thailand experience was a realization of a promise I made as a young person. For example, I saw a Tarzan movie that was made in Thailand and Clearwater, Florida. On that day, I made a promise to myself that someday, I would visit Thailand. September 1966, I was in Thailand.

For a 23 year old rural person, the Thai population were as friendly and helpful as the citizens of my hometown, London, Kentucky. However, the terrain, customs, food, indigenous clothing, holidays, etc. did not bear any resemblance to Kentucky. Equally important, the Thai Government and people accepted our country's presence with open hearts and minds. Yes, the Thai Government benefited from our military's presence but the United States benefited more. For example, the Thai Government sought the assistance for the U.S. Special Forces to train their special forces and the Central Intelligence Agency's Special Guerilla Units. The Thai Special Forces, artillery units and Special Guerilla Units were contracted by the U.S Central Intelligence Agency to assist Laotian and Meo (Muang) Armies fight the Pathet Lao, North Vietnamese and Chinese in the Kingdom of Laos.

Our country's mission in Thailand and former French Indo-China Countries were the backbone of U.S. early involvement in South Vietnam. On the military airfield, the United States Army had a large fleet of transport aircraft used to fly logistics to South Vietnam and support the U.S. Special Forces training mission in Thailand. (For example, barrels of Agent Orange, plus the color series came in to Thailand via ship. From the port they were trucked to Don Muang. From Don Muang most were Air transported to the site for spraying. Some were trucked up-country by the transportation section of the air base using the chemicals. The United States Air Force had a KC-135 air refueling aircraft, to support U.S. bombing raids over Laos and North Vietnam. The U.S. Navy had A-3Bs that conducted super sensitive flights over non-friendly territory. U.S. C-130 ferried all newly assigned personnel from Don Muang to their up-country bases, USO entertainers came through Don Muang en route to forward locations. Jane Mansfield put two helmets over her breast. Hugh O'Brien (Wyatt Earp) brought his dance team, Bob Hope and others also came through Don Muang. On one occasion, Colonel Chappie James and Colonel Robin Olds, both Vietnam War Aces, flew in to Don Muang to pick up a load of meat for their base.

On the civilian side of the airfield, the U.S. Air Force maintained cocked F-102 air defense aircraft. These aircraft were asked to destroy and/or force to land any unknown aircraft penetrating Thai Airspace or divert them from entering into Thailand's Air Defense Identification Zone. One pilot that responded to an unidentified aircraft was shot down and killed prior to the 1973 release of the U.S. Prisoners of War.

Don Muang and other Joint Thai/U.S. Air Bases maintained air resources critical for the protection and maintenance of a U.S. Radar Site in Laos. The site was manned by American military personnel in civilian clothing and without benefit of military recognition with some contract third country nationals. The site was over-run in March 1968 by Pathet Lao and North Vietnamese military. (Project 404).

Regarding the Army's fleet of transport aircraft, we learned recently through a Department of Veteran Affairs Report the areas and dates of spraying in Cambodia, Laos, South Vietnam and Thailand. Army aircraft transported the barrels of death and disability from Don Muang to the airfields where the aircraft originated that sprayed the jungles and countryside. Equally disgusting, a VA report tells the indigenous population would somehow obtain the toxic barrels, and use them as drums to hold vehicle fuel and other uses. So, besides the direct air spraying, citizens were getting a dose of the herbicides walking down the road or driving their vehicles.

The utilization of Don Muang was the ideal location to run secret flights in support of the war. The American people and most members of Congress did not know Clandestine operations in former French Indo-China were being conducted in violation of the Geneva Accords.

Bangkok had a large harbor to support international shipping, adequate roadways and trucking companies. The distance from the port to Don Muang was not mileage prohibited. Also, there was another important Thai Shipping Port, which was a good distance South of Bangkok.

Air Operations at Don Muang were very active plus the take-offs and landings on the Bangkok International Airport side made the runways at Bangkok International Airport one of the busiest in Southeast Asia. We had our fair amount of pre-takeoff and in-flight emergencies at the airport. For example, one of the most noteworthy emergency involved a U.S. Air Force KC-135 heavily loaded, taking off to one of the Anchor Refueling Tracks in support of American bombers and fighters en-route to Laos and North Vietnam. Shortly after take-off, the floors of the tanker began to buckle for whatever the reason (I don't remember). The crew declared an emergency, dumped fuel in the local pattern, and when reaching a safe landing weight, the aircraft landed. At touch-down, the crew exited the aircraft while it was still rolling. One of the crew members suffered severe rope burns while exiting, utilizing a safety rope.

Not all the air traffic from Don Muang was hostile combat related. In addition to the visit of the President and Mrs. Johnson, Jane Mansfield, Bob Hope, Hugh O'Brien and his singers and dancers, we had U.S. Military personnel that were celebrities in their own right. For example, General Wilson, Colonel Chappie James, and Colonel Robin Olds. (Wilson was the 13th Air Force Commander known as sundown. If a commander was doing his or her job, Wilson would give them to sundown to vacate their office (allegedly). James and Olds were combat aces.

Being from Southeast Kentucky where religious teachings are as important as a primary education, I found the assignment at Don Muang troubling. Why? Our government was lying to the American people about the war in Southeast Asia. The lives of the aircrew crews departing and, hopefully returning, from flights to the northern territories of Thailand. North Vietnam and South Vietnam weighed heavily on my mind. I wondered about the indigenous civilians that were being killed, wounded and mentally injured through our military missions.

To be more specific about the troubling aircrew situation, I will explain. In the air traffic control vocation, when a pilot submit's a flight plan for his or her departure from your airfield, you review the flight plan to make sure the routes are correct, what standard instrument departure, whether VFR/IFR/DVFR. Crews orders are attached, weight and balance has to be completed and approved. NOTAMSA checked, and flight will comply with the provisions of both the classified and non-classified foreign clearance guides. When the flight plan has been approved, the aircraft dispatcher will send the flight plan to the Air Routing Traffic Control Centers (ARTCC), and the proposed flight will penetrate that country's Air Defense Identification Zone (ADIZ). The purpose is to address ARTCC to plan aircraft separation for their airspace and notify the inbound airport of the pending arrival.

There is another type of ARTCC policy which affected me most was/is the ALTRAV (altitude reservation). (My concern was realized on several occasions in the Kingdom of Laos when I could see the B-52 using the same airspace route to and from North Vietnam). What an ALTRAV does, is to reserve airspace between a certain latitude and longitude for specific dates and times. Since North Vietnam is a member state of the International Civil Aviation Organization, the North Vietnamese knew where and when U.S. Bombers would strike targets inside North Vietnam.

What did the North Vietnamese do with this information? They notified pending targets, alerted ground to air missiles of inbound targets, and knew when to scramble their MIG interceptors. So, in my opinion, ICAO notification was responsible for many shoot-downs and the deaths of many monkeys, elephants, and destruction of jungle foliage. The munitions could not be returned to home airbase, they had to be dropped. (Oh, I made my concerns known, but I was an enlisted person.)

All days were not duty days in Bangkok. Since I worked shifts, I had the opportunity to visit the many tourist sites, learned Thai history, and, of course, night life with the beautiful Thai/Thai Chinese women. (I was separated from my wife, almost knowing we would divorce, she didn't enter the picture. However, I had concerns for my daughter, but knew my mother-in-law would provide the right care for her-she did). I made the rounds to the clubs, etc. but my primary interest was with a Thai/ Chinese woman that worked at the air base as a telephone operator. Her English was outstanding, she was beautiful to my eyes, and extremely intelligent. We went to see American, Chinese and Thai movies, (War & Peace), went on dates, and naturally, were sexually involved.

If I was scheduled to meet her at her dwelling, she would always have watermelon, melons, and other fruit under ice for me to eat. I was spoiled.

Our involvement lasted only a few months, but prior to our separation she told me she was pregnant. She further advised me I should make an attempt to reconcile with my wife because of my daughter. I gave her money to purchase a sewing machine and accessories to start a sewing business as a second job. However, prior to leaving Thailand, I learned she had been dating a telephone technician where she worked, and continued to write him in the United States.

Soon after I was on-station at Kelly Air Force Base, Texas, I received a letter from my aunt in Michigan and enclosed was a letter from my Thai friends. Included was a photograph of a baby girl. Not knowing for sure, I thought the baby might be mine. So at one assignment after my divorce, I sent her and the baby airfare to join me. She declined. So from 1967 forward, I thought I might be the father of a daughter. (The baby, Monica Ann was listed to share my death benefits.) In 2006, she contacted me via telephone and e-mail, as we did have a good relationship. Finally, she told me I was not the father. The real father was a German businessman that her father was conducting business with in the Chinese section of Bangkok. (I immediately notified the air force to take the alleged daughter from my next of kin record).

Earlier I mentioned a Thai General. While in Bangkok, a Thai Prince (also a pilot) and a British Group started up a new airline in Thailand called "AIR SIAM". (The prince had fought the Japanese during their occupation of Siam (changed to Thailand). The airline was hiring personnel to which I submitted a resume to the British Director of Operations for employment. I also spoke to the general about my chances. He advise me not to attempt employment as the Thai government was not in political strife. Sure enough, the Thai Government took over the new airline and retained Air Siam's logo and other parts of their successful business. The country retains Thai International as their national air carrier.

Several paragraphs back, when I said the word lying; you would have to have spent the number of years in the different Southeast Asian countries to see what our government is responsible for in Southeast Asia. Oh, I bought the governments spin regarding the Domino Theory. In fact, I wrote a letter to my hometown newspaper, the Sentinel-Echo, to support the Vietnam War. Now for the truth.

From personal experience with Cambodians, Laotians and Vietnamese they did not and do not care about the name of their government. What they do care about and would fight till death for, and did, was the right to have a family life, work, travel, and to be a human being. Communism can not work in Southeast Asia.

In all fairness to our government, the ideal one government, economic system, and/or government system could control Southeast Asia is viable. For example, in Vietnam, Cambodia, Laos, Philippines, South Vietnam, and Thailand's major cities it is the Chinese merchants controlling the economy. (Nothing new. The Chinese are like Zionist, they see themselves as superior to other citizens/residents of the countries in which they reside). After the United States departed Vietnam, the Vietnamese force Chinese merchants from Vietnam, which resulted in a short term exchange of artillery fire between China and Vietnam.

Speaking of China and the Chinese. On or about December 28, 2006, former Senator and presidential candidate, Mr. John Edwards, told Hard Ball Host, Mr. Chris Matthews, our government should focus on China instead of spending all its capital on the Middle East. Mr. Edwards is correct. For example, the Chinese built a super highway, with radar controlled artillery pieces, down through Laos to Thailand during the 1970s, coupled with the highway and the Chinese merchants, Southeast Asia will be dominated economically for sure and may even be politically controlled by China.

On a more personal note, while in Bangkok, I was a Christian of sort, well I had not reached the Atheist stage as I am today. In fact, I went to the Bangkok Grace Baptist Church several times and met many wonderful American and Thai families., (Didn't go to hear about God just to be with my fellow Americans and seek advise of the pastor). The reason for the advise dealt with my wife and daughter.

My wife forbid me writing to my daughter, returned my mothers letters and gifts, and caused me trouble whenever she could. To this end, I became extremely frustrated, agitated, and having numbness of the right hand side of my body, especially my face. Still to this date, I do not know If it's the mental stress over my family situation or the fact the Congress of the United States did not know what the U.S. Military was doing in Southeast Asia and/or exposure to toxic agents stored on the flight line. (Congress's leadership knew but not the entire House or Senate).

To deal with the numbness, I went on sick call. The air base didn't have the equipment to x-ray my head so I was sent to the Thai Hospital located on the air base. The U.S. physician wrote a prescription for anti-depressants, plus I spoke with Grace Church's pastor. The pastor was wise in that I could do no more than I could. However, the only way I could correct for myself, the war doubts, was to write a member of Congress. I did. A waste of time.

Oh advise from and old Sergeant. As I wrote, I was no longer an active Christian, so I had intercourse with a number of females before the lady I addressed. The advise if you see warts in the female's pubic area, get up, put your pants on and leave. The warts are called VD warts. I had to have some removed at Don Muang. Also the doctor reprimanded me for a wart on the top of my head. I did not argue with him, the head wart had been their since I was a teenager. I always thought the wart was the results of my older sister hitting me on the head with a piece of wood.

I did, some years after in-patient surgery provide an answer to a subject regarding VD warts. I was home on leave. My younger sister told me her baby sitter told her that she had warts in the pubic area. I told my sister they were VD warts, and she needed to have them removed. A lesson from Thailand.

My next assignment was Kelly Air Force Base, Texas. The day I departed Bangkok, my lady friend was not present. Just another day in the life of an Airman.

Texas

By now the transfer process was almost routine. At least this time, I was being assigned to the Air Force Logistics Command (AFLC). Command Headquarters was at Wright Patterson Air Force Base, Dayton, Ohio. No bombers, no tankers, and no ICBM in their silos. The Command had civilians doing many of the tasks an enlisted person would accomplish on a Strategic Air Command or Tactical Air Command Base. We were charged with maintaining the logistics for the air frames.

We will start with my arrival in London, Kentucky, to visit my Mother and Sisters. The time spent with my immediate family was great, as always. Because one had to speak softly around my Wife (still married), my Mother had asked my younger Sister if I still loved her. Pam's answer was yes. Mom had been a Mother, Father, friend, and the rock I could, and did stand on from time to time. She wasn't a high school graduate. She had outstanding math skills, which she taught to me and my Sisters. She wasn't afraid of anyone or anything. Short fuse and temper - yes.

For some reason my Wife, Daughter, and Mother-in-law, resided in Winter Haven, Florida. The state where I met and married my Wife.

Wow! My Daughter was beautiful, and extremely intelligent. My Mother-in-law was the same sweet, understanding woman that I cherished before spousal separation, and did until the day of her death. My Wife had not changed. She took me to a bar, where she apparently hung out. She told me of a meeting with an individual that had asked her to be a bit player in a pornographic movie. I don't know if she was a participant of not, as it would not have mattered. However her attitude, and view of the real world had not changed. Our marriage was over. Goodbye to my Daughter and Mother-in-law.

On to the airport for a flight to San Antonio, Texas, and a bus trip to Kelly Air Force Base.

The assignment to Kelly Air Force Base was an ideal position for an air operations person. The base was an Air Force Logistic Command Base, which meant civilian employees in most operations slots, especially in the flight records section (I had no experience in the maintenance of aircrew records, or the many facets involved, assuring that a pilot met his flight requirements). I was excited.

As always, when life starts to look good, something ugly raises it's head. The head this time was a Notice of Divorce from a South Carolina Court (You may recall, my spouse was a resident of Winter Haven, Florida). Naturally, I did not have the funds to travel to Hampton, South Carolina to meet the court date. The Air Force came through. I went to Kelly's Air Force Aid Society. The society loaned me the money to travel, and secure a lawyer.

I flew to Charleston, South Carolina, and stayed with my Wife's Aunt and Uncle (My Wife was staying with this Aunt when my Daughter was born in a Charleston Military Hospital).

The period of stay in South Carolina was spent with my Wife's relatives in Charleston, South Carolina. I had better rapport with them than I had with my Wife.

Following an overnight with the relatives, I rented an automobile, and drove to Hampton. After a short period of arrival, I met the attorney that I hired via telephone, while in Texas. The next person I met was her attorney, and alleged lover, while she remained in Florida.

The two attorneys worked out an agreement, which I signed. Per the divorce, I would pay for her automobile (which I was already doing), pay child support (no objections), assure my Daughter's dependent rights for medical, dental, commissary, base exchange, plus the many other advantages a military dependent is entitled (Again, no objections).

To assure my Daughter's access to clothing , so she would fit in with her peers, I established a Sears Credit Card account for my Daughter. Big Mistake! My Wife used the card to purchase items for nieces and nephews, as well as my Daughter. I cancelled the account.

With a terrible situation resolved, or so I thought, I returned to Kelly Air Base. Yes, Kelly's operations slots were indeed filled by civilian employees, but to my surprise, I was charged with On-The-Job Training for six airman (Each of the airman had been in at least one Air Force specialty, prior to being assigned to the Air Operations Career Field). You may recall, I cross-trained myself.

Recognizing the task before me, I wrote study material to supplement issued training literature, tests (for in-office testing), and conducted classroom training in the afternoons, three days per week.

Of the six airman, two posed additional problems for me. One airman, older than me, had hearing and learning (retaining knowledge) difficulties, the other was simply a goof-off. To assure their ability to learn the air operations specialty, I wrote the Squadron Commander and asked that he have the squadron, charge of quarters, monitor the two individuals each evening for a set number of hours. My training program succeeded. All six airman passed their vocational skills test.

At the time of my training program, and Air Force policy, the Air Operations Career Field was divided into two separate areas of possible assignments. One was base operations, and/or Command and Control Section (Command Post). The second was Flight Records and/or Aircraft Scheduling.

The stress factor was that during your entire career, you may never work in both areas of vocational knowledge. However, your testing for promotion contained questions from all areas of the Air Force specialty. Additionally, before I could achieve the rank for Air Operations Superintendent, I had to be proficient in both the air traffic and administrative areas of the Air Operations Career.

Fortunately, there were other Non-Commissioned Officers that addressed the question with Air Force Headquarters. Finally, after a number of years explaining our view, the specialty was divided into two separate but equal vocations.

Prior to my reassignment to another air base, the airman with hearing and learning difficulties received notification to transfer to Tan Son Hut Air Base, Republic of South Vietnam. I immediately contacted base personnel, and the Flight Surgeon's Office at Wilford Hall Air Force Hospital (A couple of our line pilots were also flight surgeons assigned to Wilford Hall).

Yes, the medical results reported his medical disability, but the needs of the Air Force outweighed common sense. When under my supervision, he worked in the flight records section, in which he did an outstanding job. I knew he would be unable to work in the stressful, split second, decision area of air operations.

I learned later, the airman was unable to perform his duties in air operations in Vietnam, and was what?

A true benefit of being a supervisor at Kelly, was the base provided off-base apartments, Billy Mitchell Village. The apartments were within a short walking distance from the air base. Amenities were the responsibility of the occupants, such as telephone service, television, and any other electrical appliance.

One of the residents that shared the apartment with me was a Command and Control Technician. He was assigned to the base's command post. He, like myself, had been assigned to the Kingdom of Thailand, but an air base up-country. In fact, our personal lives in-country emulated each other pretty closely. He was married, but had a Thai girlfriend. His wife had an affair, but became pregnant with her Jody. My ex-wife told me on several occasions, that I was not the father of my daughter. Although, I never had a DNA test, I knew then, as I know now, that she was lying. Also, unlike my question of reuniting with my wife at my return, he was desperate to re-join his wife regardless of the pregnancy. Unfortunately, as is too often the case, his Mother, in Alabama, did not want her son to take his wife back. When he drank, which was often, he complained of his mother's demands, and remained in love with his wife.

Having gone through a messy divorce, my advise to him was if he loved his wife, then go back to her. He was married to her, not to his mother. I clearly understood his despair and mental stress.

Although we shared the same apartment, we were never close. However, one period of time, he did not return to the apartment for a day or so. I learned that he was in the mental section of the Wilford Hospital following treatment for a motor vehicle accident.

Allegedly, he was en-route to Mexico, the country, to seek companionship with a prostitute, when the accident occurred. While in the emergency room, he informed the hospital staff of his intent to take his own life. Naturally he was detained, hospitalized, and interviewed before being released back to duty.

One afternoon, I returned to quarters and turned on the television to watch the evening news. The telephone rang. The party calling was the on-duty supervisor at the command post, inquiring about the status of my apartment mate. He was scheduled for duty, but failed to report. I told the caller to hold on, and I would check his room. I knocked several times, but no response. Knowing the severity of possible AWOL charges, I opened the door slightly, and observed him lying on the bed. I walked into the room, calling his name, and at his bedside I reached down and shook his arm. His arm was cold and stiff. A pistol was lying by his right side. I declared a vulgar statement, and told the caller that he was dead. I then called the local police.

During the follow-up of his death, I learned he had purchased the weapon for his mother, and in fact, had it wrapped to be mailed. Instead of mailing it, he had opened the package, took out the weapon, and killed himself. I also learned that he had gone into my room and took a bottle of Rum. My supervisor, Chief of Operations, asked me if I wanted days off because of his death, I refused.

More firsts for me. The Kelly assignment was the first station where an American of color was under my supervision. The person was a Staff Sergeant and Cross-Trainee. I had worked for a black supervisor in South Korea, shared quarters, dated black women, and worked alongside Black Americans from day one in the Air Force. My supervisor tasks were enlightening to say the least, plus the position brought an unknown impression by others to my attention.

Addressing the Sergeant. One day at work, the Sergeant told me there was a death in his family, and needed some personal time to travel out of state. Since aircrew members usually took a seventy-two hour break after returning from an overnighter or longer, I told the Sergeant that he could have three days off. Alas, during his absence, one of the rated officers asked where the Sergeant was, and I replied that he was off. The officer became upset and went to see my Colonel. The Colonel asked me what the situation was, and I explained. The Colonel sided with me.

Over a period of time, I met the Sergeant's wife and family. In fact, his wife owned and managed a restaurant in the San Antonio metro area, where on at least one occasion I ate. Following a meal at his wife's establishment, the Sergeant turned to me and stated, "Sarge, you're prejudiced but fair." Wow! Was I shocked. His words went through my mind for days afterwards. I knew then, and know now, that I am no prejudiced.

To get an answer for the statement for myself, I thought back at my history with different races in the United States, and the International community. It was true, that I had never had a close relationship with a Black American Male, outside the barracks or work area, except for supervisor in Korea (We drank together at the NCO Club a few times). Childhood association was in London with a Black family that did commercial plumbing. Contact was only at the construction site. The first seven years of my military career found that all my personal friends were white, not by choice, but through my personal environment. I was a nerd, and did not participate in any sports, and associated with one person. The person was from Mississippi. We were assigned together in Florida and Korea (dated his wife before they were married), slept with his sister-in-law, and visited each other families as family members. His children called me Uncle and my son called him Uncle. Naturally, I knew more people, but personal association was rare, mostly just official functions. Also, the time period was the 1960s, when our country wa somewhat segregated.

My mind was still confused, the logic of non-association did not wash. There had to be something else. I knew it wasn't the use of profanity, use of racial slurs, or any inherent practice from my home environment (My Mother did not allow profanity, name calling, or refusal to welcome another human being to our home).

Being that I had truly mixed ancestry maybe would rule out prejudice. This reasoning didn't wash. Finally, the only possible fault in presenting myself to others, I concluded, was my feelings of inferiority.

On a personal and pleasing note, after my divorce, I started seeking companionship from the many beautiful women around Kelly Air Force Base, Lackland Air Force Base, and San Antonio. I was lucky, I met this beautiful, intelligent, American woman, my age, around the apartment complex. She was of Mexican ancestry, and she seemed not concerned about my mixed ancestry. She had an older model car, but it ran well. Over a period of time, we came to know each other, and enjoy each other's company. On one date, we planned a picnic, and day outing at a famous Texas Park located in New Braunwells, Texas.

Prejudice was still rampant in Texas. At the entrance of the park was a sign demeaning Americans of non-European ancestry, but we never felt any hard feelings against us, or anyone attempt to shun us. We had a wonderful day that consisted of laying on a beach blanket under the Texas sun (her in her two piece bathing suit). We rode the pedal boats in the park's water system and enjoyed each other. The day was/is the most enjoyable day of remembrance that I have of my assignment at Kelly Air Force Base.

In an earlier chapter, I wrote about the Thai woman I met at Don Muang, who later came to the United States. Because of my feelings for her, and her for me I believe, I will provide more information. The letter I identified earlier was post marked in Old Saybrook, Connecticut. She was living with the Mother of her boyfriend that worked at the base's telephone inside plant. We corresponded for awhile, then she married the telephone technician. On occasions, we would speak to each other, and I would ask her if I could come to Connecticut to see the baby girl. She said no. The husband was now a police officer, and vowed to kill me. Finally, in 2006, my question was answered, I was not the father of the girl.

In approximately June or July 1968, I received notification of a pending assignment to a classified location. The assignment required a "TOP SECRET CLEARANCE", civilian clothing (I received a voucher for clothing), Diplomatic Passport, and an outstanding military record. Furthermore, within a short time of the assignment notification, I was ordered to report for temporary duty to Lackland Air Force Base, Texas, to attend the Air Police's Combat School.

Having been a graduate of the Strategic Air Command's Tough Tiger Training, I looked forward to the school (I was 24 now, versus 17 at the time of the previous training). The Air Force had built a replica Vietnamese village that would be filled with smoke, and we would go through the village. On the trails, we would encounter concussion grenades, blowing up water and surface debris. We were introduced to different weaponry, and the art of throwing a hand grenade. Also, as in Tough Tiger, each person had to be in the position of Point Person.

Comically to me, one afternoon our group was resting when an instructor threw a grenade into our group. The others scattered, I picked up the grenade and threw it back to the instructor. As the Point Person, I located the trip wire across the trail, and asked the instructor to disarm the explosive. The instructor said no. I turned and told the person behind me about the trip wire, and asked him to relay the same information to the person behind him. Alas, within a few seconds, the trip wire was tripped. If we had been in a combat environment, a number of us would have been killed or wounded, plus the enemy would have known exactly where we were located.

The group had no respect for war, and lacked the discipline to survive in a hostile environment. The incident reminded me of former Senator Max Cleland, who became an amputee from duties in South Vietnam. His injury was caused by a fellow soldiers grenade falling from the person's clothing or hand.

Upon completion of Indo-China, and weapons training at Lackland, I returned to my air operations duties. I learned that Ray Charles and the Rayletts were going to perform in San Antonio. I asked the Air Operations Commander's Secretary if she would go with me. She agreed. Wow! What a show. I had good friends at Kelly.

I would be amiss if I didn't write something about the mission of our organization at Kelly. An interesting story pertains to the unveiling and launching of the C-5A, at the manufacturing plant in Georgia. The

Generals, Commanders, and Political, all convened in Georgia to watch the largest aircraft in the U.S. Air Force inventory roll out of the hangar (I went onboard one of the base aircraft to serve as a steward to and from Kelly). As the C-5A was taxiing, one of the landing gear wheels came off. The Honorable (now deceased) L. Mendel River, Congressman from South Carolina, reportedly said something to the effect, that there was no problem as the aircraft had 28 wheels.

Our organization owned C-54, C118, T-29 and T-39 aircraft to support our overseas, and domestic aircraft delivery commitments to the Department of Defense Customers. I recall some assistance in the delivery of an updated P-61 Mustang World War II fighter to a Latin American country.

On weekends, I used to hitch a ride with the pilots that were flying to remain proficient, and retain their flight pay. Besides the rated pilots, we had navigators, and rated flight surgeons. We would leave Kelly on Friday, and return on Sunday. I truly enjoyed the flights, plus I learned more about air traffic control. Equally interesting on one mission, the aircraft commander allowed me to sit in the left seat, and control the T-39.

A few months prior to my departure from Kelly, I received word that I had been promoted to Technical Sergeant (E-6), but would not receive my stripe until I was at my next assignment. Also, I learned that I would be receiving an Air Force Commendation Medal for my On-The-Job Training Program. The award was presented by the Air Attache in Laos.

Kingdom Of Loas

My routine for travel overseas was the same as past assignments, however, this time I would be traveling in civilian clothing, My orders read Classified Southeast Asia location.

On approach at Bangkok International/Don Muang Royal Thai Air Base, Kingdom of Thailand, looking out the aircraft's window, the landscape was the same as in 1966-1967.

When we disembarked, due to our diplomatic passports, we were met by officials from the United States Military Advisory Group (MAG). We were given our choice of hotels to remain overnight. I chose the first hotel, as I was extremely familiar with the neighborhood.

After checking into my room, and cleaning up a bit, I went to the snack bar to have Thai Sweet and Sour Beef (good food). After eating, I stood out in the street (sidewalk) for awhile to breath the once familiar Thai air. Knowing the long, unknown days before me and the others, I went to my room to sleep, and await a new day.

The following morning, we were picked up, and taken to our in-country headquarters, the Capitol Hotel (Our real headquarters was Headquarters Command, Washington, D.C.). At the headquarters, we did the normal in-processing, but with an extremely different stance this time. We turned in our military identification cards, dog tags, Geneva Convention Card, military drivers license, and any other items identifying us as members of the United States Air Force., We were no longer identified by military rank, but we were called "Mister."

When I became "Good To Go", another member of the project was ready to go as well. The other members Top Secret Clearances had not been finalized. We loaded into a MAG vehicle, and headed down the heavily congested, fume filled road to the Bangkok International Airport (The trip brought back memories of Thai Bus #29). At the airport, we bypassed customs, etc., and went straight to a beautiful, shiny silver DC-3 (C-47) aircraft. The aircraft had no markings, other than the tail number 933. The aircraft belonged to an organization known as "Air America". (Christopher Robbins wrote a book titled "Air America", which was about the airline that transported us to the Kingdom of Laos.) The other large framed passenger with me had the nickname of "HOSS".

At precisely the Estimated Time of Departure (ETD), the aircraft's wheels were in the well, and we were en-route to a divided nation at war (The exact departure reminded me of the pilots from the U.S. Air Forces Strategic Air Command-on time takeoffs). Two brothers (half brothers actually), were the leaders of the parties at war: The Royal Laotian Military and the Communist Pathet Lao Forces. The war was an extension of the Vietnam War raging across the border from Laos.

About thirty minutes from Laos, the aircraft made an approach, and landed at one of the U.S./Thai Air Bases in Thailand-Udorn Royal Thai Air Base. Udorn was a major trans-shipment center for Air America to supply Laos, and other parts of the region with necessary items to sustain the Laotian Air and Ground War. Business completed by the aircrew, and once again we were airborne, heading to cross the infamous Mekong River and the Royal Kingdom of Laos.

Touchdown at the Vientiane International Airport. Taxiing to our disembarking area, we could see vintage Royal Laotian Air Force (RLAF) C-47 aircraft, H-34 helicopters, 0-1, and U-17 aircraft. The U.S. Embassy's C-47 aircraft was also parked on the ramp (These aircraft were given to the Laotian Government by former President Dwight David Eisenhower, with the understanding that once an aircraft was destroyed, the airplane would not be replaced). The individuals that met us were from the U.S. Air Attache Office (AIRA). We loaded our gear, and ourselves into a U.S. Government vehicle. The vehicle had CD plates, which meant our vehicle was a U.S. Embassy Diplomatic Vehicle (diplomatic license tags).

Driving from the airport to the city, we passed the Air America, Continental Air Services, and others compounds. Further down the road, we went by a vacant French School compound, and near the school was an excellent Korean Restaurant. Continuing on, we passed Gold Ships, Indian Tailor Shops, local bars and clubs. Our trip ended as we pulled into the U.S. Defense Attaches Offices compound.

The U.S. Army's Attache and support offices were in front of the building, the Air Attache's and support offices were in the rear, and attached near the Attache's Office, was the U.S. Army's civilian contracted communication center.

The Air Attache's structure was in dire need of repair. So much so, that asbestos was sticking out of the walls, and air/heating vents. So a decision was made to build a new Air Attache Building, and what a building it was or is. It looked like a giant white bunker, built to reflect rounds fired at the building. However, prior to moving to the new structure, the old building suffered from a terrible Vientiane Flood. The airport, lower sections of the city, and the Vientiane Plains were all flooded. The Mekong overran it's banks by miles. Even with sand bags at the door's entrance, I sat in water up to my ankles, while operating the command and control center's radios and telephone switchboard.

After I departed Laos, I read were Marine Embassy Guards were assigned to the Air Attache Building. Apparently one Marine, Bill Kulp, received some news media coverage, by not allowing Communist officials to enter the building.

As always, I was in-processing. After processing, I was taken to my residence. My new home, I would be sharing with the senior Air Force enlisted person (if their were any American military). The villa was designed and built, by either the French of Euro-Asians in Vientiane. Also, the house had a rooftop patio, surrounded by a walled fence, and of course, there was an embassy contracted guard.

This residence, along with a dozen or so more, were leased by the U.S. Embassy to house Americans working in the Kingdom. Prior to my arrival, my housemate hired a wonderful woman of Cambodian and Vietnamese ancestry, as his cook, maid, and housekeeper. Together we paid her salary. The housekeeper resided, along with her Laotian female helper, in the maid quarters at the back of the villa.

Since there was an on-going war between Laotian government troops, and Communist led Pathet Lao (Lao Country) forces, Laos was under Martial Law and curfew. Although the major cities, and most provinces were under the administrative control of the Royal Laotian Government located in Vientiane.

The Royal Capital and the King's residence were at Luang Prabang.

During my time in-country, Laos was a constitutional monarchy. The King was head of state, and supreme religious leader. When I went back in 1974, on temporary duty, the King of Laos was no longer king.

He was forced from the throne in 1973. Of interest, because the Communist (Pathet Lao) were legally part of the government of Laos, and the Pathet Lao/North Vietnamese/Chinese forces had defeated U.S. backed forces.

The Pathet Lao had a compound about a mile from my residence. Some days you could drive by the compound, and the compound would be empty. Later, you would see individuals out working in their small garden, or playing some type of sport. I suppose Vientiane was the Recreation and Relaxation (R&R) location for Pathet Lao fighters

(Noteworthy, the enemies they were fighting were: the United States, Royal Laotian government forces, Meo tribesman, and contracted aircrews).

On more than one occasion, controllers under my supervision were asked to leave the club or bar they were visiting, because Pathet Lao soldiers would come into the facility.

The Kingdom of Laos was divided in to five military regions. They were Vientiane (Administrative Capital), Long Tieng (CIA, General Vang Pao (MEOs), Ravens), Luang Probing (Royal Capital), Pakse (CIA, Ravens), Savannakhet (CIA, Ravens).

Pakse and Savnnakhet were once Royal Kingdoms ruled by different royal families. (Sadly, there was another site, mentioned in the Bangkok Chapter, but the site was over-run. Air strikes were called in to destroy the structures).

At each region was an American Air Operations Center Commander, support staff and U.S. Forward Air Controllers (FAC) call sign RAVEN. Our mission (Vientiane was the senior controlling station) was to train Royal Laotian Air Force (RLAF) officers and enlisted personnel while the RAVEN FAC located enemy targets, marked the target and called in U.S., Lao, Meo, and contracted aircrews to destroy the target.

Laos was our Spain, the RAVEN FAC were active in the research and development of better and weapons delivery. For example, weapons, sensitive devices, etc., were tested in Laos prior to being assigned to U.S. inventory. The FACs would mark the site or target with smoke, then whatever was to be delivered struck the point identified by the Raven.

My duty position was as the individual in charge of the Air Attache's Command and Control Center. (If in the real air force, my title would have been Non-Commissioned Officer in Charge of the Air Attahce's Command & Control Center). The mission of the Air Attache, besides his intelligence duties as part of the Defense Intelligence Agency (DIA), was the direct control of all U.S. Air Force resources assigned in Laos or entering Laotian airspace. In this light, we were involved in Search and Rescue missions of downed aircrew members or special forces teams, involved with the Central Intelligence Agency for all insertions and extractions of allied special guerilla forces, the control and safety monitor for the U.S. military sites located in 4 of 5 Laotian provinces and, believe me, much, much more. On the non-combat side, we assisted foreign embassies and Laotian government personnel with selected travel, air support in case of floods and other emergencies, and whatever action directed by the U.S. Ambassador to Laos.

The United States Embassy was the only embassy that possessed an aircraft in-country. The aircraft transported the Russian Ambassador and other dignitaries to Thailand's Annual Elephant Jamboree. Provided humanitarian support to the local Catholic priest and his parish. The aircraft had a secret panel or door on the belly of the airplane to take photographs of interesting sites during over flight.

After hours, I was on-call to respond to emergencies at the Forward Operating Locations, transmit and receive intelligence reports to and from sites, plus transmit air operations (FRAG) orders issued by 7th Air Force Headquarters. The FRAG identified all the air sorties scheduled to strike the enemy and/or support infiltrations/extractions, and the transmission of sorties the RAVEN Forward Air Controllers would control in their military region. Also, the command center contained the secure and non-secure communication devices that monitored the management of logistics and munitions expended by Laotian, Moung, and American pilots. Equally important, we were the reception center for three Americans released by the North Vietnamese to American Control.

Moreover, should an emergency exist and/or enemy convoys/personnel were observed by contract Forward Air Guides (FAG), I would be contracted by the duty controller. In turn, I would come into the center, advise the duty officer at home and the 7th Air Force Control Center (Saigon) for the diversion of air resources required to assist the FAG or destroy the target.

To alleviate the necessity for the Air Operations Officer to come into the command center during curfew to sign out-going message forms, I recommended that a pony circuit be installed between the Air Attache's Command Center and the Army's Communication Center. (At this date, the Air Attache had moved into a new, multi-story, concrete bunker type facility, a fairly good distance from the communications center). The installation allowed the controllers or myself to cut a teletype tape of the message form text, and then transmit the tape via secure Crypto pony circuit to the message center. (Message forms were pre-signed and the operations officer briefed prior to dispatch). The communication center would, in turn, make a copy of the tape, add headers or whatever required by the center, and send out the message. Equally beneficial and assured safety, the pony circuit eliminated the need for our personnel to walk into a hostile environment carrying Top Secret and SI traffic to the message center.

Earlier, I mentioned the duty controller contacting me and on some occasions, the older American from the villa, to assist in the transmission on the FRAG. One night, I was contacted regarding an urgent message from a FAG. At this point in the assignment, I had a live-in girlfriend and my own private residence. I went outside and got into a vehicle, mine or the governments, I don't remember, and headed toward the command center. Mind you this trip was without a curfew pass. Just as I was about to enter an area near the Pathet Lao Compound, I saw an up-coming Laotian Military Police roadblock. The police were well armed with a large caliber automatic weapon mounted on a jeep. What made matters worse, the soldiers were not sober. I explained my situation in broken Lao/Thai and English and allowed to proceed. Disgusting is the fact the Laotian government offered the U.S. Embassy (Air Attache included) a specific number of curfew passes. If we received any I don't know, as the officers probably took all of them. I know I didn't get one.

Returning to the FAG incident. After arriving in the command post, the duty controller said that a FAG had spotted a convoy of Communist vehicles and tanks traveling down the road. Having obtained the coordinates and FAG's call sign and radio frequency, I contacted 7th Air Force to divert resource to strike the targets. The tasked support aircraft checked in with the command post, and we provided the information we had. Not only did the aircrews copy but apparently the Communist forces.

The FAG informed us that before the strike aircraft arrived, the potential targets parked near an abandoned structure. When the aircraft had to return to base for fuel, the communist resumed their journey south. (The aircrews had to comply with the U.S. Rules of Engagement which prohibited their ordnance release because of the structure).

To my surprise, the Chief of Operations called me into his office and told me I was going to relieve a Ground Combat Controller, at Moung Soui, for a few days while he had some time off. (I don't remember If the Lieutenant Colonel was the officer with whom I refused to redo the Controllers duty schedule so his friend could have some time off. Controllers in question were two different individuals),

Moung Soui was in communist controlled territory, there were no fixed structures at the runway was made of laterite. Of note, the site was located near the Plain De Jares in Northern Laos. The U.S. Army had two personnel, one officer and one enlisted personnel, both artillery advisors, that lived in the Moung Soui compound/cantonment. (The house location was not, repeat not, near the runway as I suggested in other writings. (Reference Mr. Moody's writings)

To prepare for tasking, I went to one of the Indian tailors in Vientiane. I had one of the work suits that some westerners wore.

The shirt and pants had zippers in different areas to provide more holding space. To familiarize myself with the transportation arrangements and things to do at the site, I accompanied the controller I was replacing to Moung Soui for a day or so. I do not remember the exact number of days,

The only problem to the director's plan was that I was not trained as a Ground Combat Controller. Yes, the specialty was in the Air Traffic Control Career Field ,but it was not my area of expertise. My knowledge was in flight planning, flight publications, NOTAMS, aircraft dispatch & scheduling from a fixed base operations facility.

Operational day came. The following days would be in an environment controlled by North Vietnamese and Pathet Lao military. Flights to and from the site beginning before daylight in Vientiane and returning to Vientiane in the evenings were themselves a hazard. Communist forces shot at, and too often, struck aircraft flying in their airspace. I'm thankful communist forces had not introduced the Strella Missile (SA-7) into war during this period.

Left my quarters early without breakfast. (I told my maid/housekeeper I would be late coming home for the next few days). When I arrived at the Air Operations Center (AOC), I went to the building and took the old Navy .38 caliber pistol and holster out of the drawer and closed the holster around my waist. I was the only one, to my knowledge, that had any type weapon. (I didn't ask for permission, I just took the weapon).

Time to load up. The aircraft mechanics and munitions specialist and I went aboard the Air America aircraft for out flight to Moung Soui.

When we arrived at the site, we all disembarked. The maintenance and munitions personnel went to their area on the apron and I went to the parked MRK108 Radio Jeeps. I started the jeep, moved into a position where I had clear vision of the runway from any direction and attached the fifty foot radio antenna to the jeep. (For the unfamiliar, the MRK-

108 is a small Willis type Jeep with a communications pallet loaded to the rear area of the Jeep. The pallet provided HF, UHF, VHF, & FM radio frequencies, plus there was teletype capability). Daylight came and we heard the roar of the T-28s inbound to the airfield. I advised the pilots that the runway was clear and they landed.

The combat pilots, American and Indigenous, were so dedicated that they remained in their aircraft, while the aircraft was refueled, and ordnance attached to the fuselage. Fuel was hand cranked out of fifty gallon drums. Munitions were mounted, for the most part, through physical power of the munitions specialist/technicians (An interesting note, the aircraft had a metal frame on each side of the aircraft, where one could change the nationality of the aircraft, depending upon where the aircraft were to bomb). My primary responsibility was to clear the aircraft to land and takeoff, and to maintain communications with the command center and sister sites.

On the first or second day, an American Air Operations Center Commander was flight lead with the RLAF pilots, which landed from a previous strike mission. The commander was upset because an enemy artillery site had opened fire on him, He reloaded along with his flight, headed for the artillery site, and returned a happy commander. He had destroyed the artillery site.

On the last day of the temporary duty, I believe. I had to fire the .38 caliber pistol that I found at the Vientiane AOC. The reason for firing the weapon, was a column of Meo refugees had walked from the forest and were crossing the runway. I suppose the column was a common practice, as communist forces had become more aggressive in their quest, and the tribesman were trying to find a safe environment (Losses among the Meos was horrific).

As fate would have it, a flight of RLAF aircraft were inbound. I yelled in English, Lao, and Thai for the Meo to go fast, and get off the runway with no response, I fired the pistol. The people turned and looked, and continued their Southward movement (Who knows if Pathet Lao or North Vietnamese were in the column. I didn't see anyone stop them, and ask for identification). The inbound aircraft landed without any people getting killed, or airframes damaged.

Late in the day, an unmarked C-130 landed in a monsoon rain. I attempted the best I could, to direct the aircraft to a parking area. There were no base personnel at the site. The C-130 stopped, the back ramp opened, and the crew chief off-loaded fifty gallon drums of what I thought was aviation fuel, but it may have been water. One of the histories I read of the Moung Soui, reported that water was flown in regularly to soak down the laterite runway. The report continued to say that Command felt it unsafe for airman to remain at the site for more than 2 or 3 days, due to blowing dust and smoke.

Behind me, and to my left, Air America H-34 helicopter crews were either off-loading or on-loading ground forces during the monsoon. In this light, I suppose to the C-130 crew, that those of us out in the Monsoon were mentally imbalanced. I had to remain with the jeep, as the helicopters were in the airport control zone (Even though they did not contact me).

Apparently a photo was taken of me, the MRK-108, and the helicopter scene. The why is, that some weeks or so later, a bar/club run by a British citizen, had a wall painting of the exact same scenario. I didn't pay any attention to the painting at the time. However, a year or so passed, and I saw the photograph in a magazine or somewhere, but again did not pay any attention. But when the VA denied my claim that I was in Laos, I attempted to find the photograph. I even wrote the Central Intelligence Agency under the Freedom of Information Act (No picture, but a nice letter from the CIA). I called a couple of offices at Hurlburt and Eglin, but no one had seen the photograph.

On a personal note, I was expecting to be struck by lightning when standing by the jeep. A monsoon rain is bad enough, but when there is lightning, one should be concerned.

The sun began to do down, and the command post had not notified me on an aircraft scheduled to pickup the AOC team, and myself. I suppose the command center, and whatever other parties that may have been listening, may have thought that I was frightened. No. I wasn't frightened, but truly concerned. We had no weapons (except for my pistol),no bunkers, no barricades, or any defensive position. After the sun had gone down, an Air American aircraft diverted to pick us up. The command center never notified us in advance. At least it was my last day at the site. The Combat Controller would assume his duties. I was back in the Command & Control Center.

The write up regarding Moung Soui were my words, as I best remember being tasked to work out of the Lima Site. The following is the Vientiane Air Operations Center's Commander's view of the same operation. More detailed:

"We were accumulating supplies, and munitions for an operation to take the western most mountains overlooking the PDJ from the NVA and the Pathet Lao. The munitions were already in place, but not built-up. About 14 of the guys from Vientiane joined the other troops that were sent to site 108 to help build up the ordnance. The Victor T-28's were scheduled to come in, and start operating the following Monday. The guys were complaining, and were upset because they were not allowed to bring weapons with them, so they could shoot-up the bad guys if they were to come. There was a real concern about whom they might shoot if, and when, any shooting started. Radios became the alternative for guns, and they were instructed to lay-low, hunker-down, hide, and don't try to be heroes if any shooting started.

The guys were also complaining because they had to stay in a large tent that had been erected in the middle of a volleyball court. The court was about 40 feet below, and between the two houses where the U.S. Army and Civilian RO and USAID representatives lived. This was to provide the troops with a ringside seat to a classic NVA sapper attack.

Moung Soui got hit the very first night after the troops arrived. Our guys were in the tent when the bad guys came, and over-ran the compound. As best as can be recalled, "Smokes", an Army Sergeant, was the first man to be shot, as he ran out of the house., The Lao interpreter, who worked for Captain Bush, and was a good kid, was shot through the shoulder as he dove out the door of the main house, because the bad guys had set it on fire.

The bad guys eventually blew up the house, and Captain Bush made a dash from the burning house, and headed toward the Western most house, where the DEPCHIEF/RO guy named Bob Parshall lived. Before he could make it, he was cut down by an AK-47, just as he made the steps to Bob's house. Time magazine ran an article with pictures shortly after the attack, about Captain Bush, the incident, and the fact that American military personnel were operating Laos. Captain Bush had been silhouetted against the side of Bob's house, making him a perfect target. The evidence of what had transpired was obvious by the blood splattered on the door to the house. Two bad guys had been very accurate, and Captain Bush was mortally wounded. Captain Bush was one on the two Army advisors that were allowed by the Geneva Accords of 1962, to advise the Neutralists at Moung Soui.

The NVA ran through the Eastern house three times shooting everything in sight, and tossing in a couple of hand grenades as he left. When the bad guys entered Bob's house, they didn't see him, as he had pulled the mattress off his bed and hid under it. Twice they entered his room, and sprayed the room with AK-47 fire, and never spotted big Bob under the mattress. It is even more astonishing, when you realize that Bob Parshall was one big man, he weighed well over 300 pounds. He was at least a minimum of 45-50 inches around the waist. How they missed seeing him, no one will ever know. Someone up there was looking out for him that night. Bob wore a name badge that had the initials S.O.B. on it (He always said that it stood for "Sweet Ole Bob"). The camp commander's wife was also beat-up pretty bad, but no harm came to the commander. His complete avoidance of any contact with the bad guys made this story very suspect.

Meanwhile, the bad guys set a satchel charge on top of the hood of the Mark 108 (Radio) jeep, which was about 20 feet away from the guys in the tent. The satchel charge blew the engine down through the jeep frame. Later the radios were jury-rigged, checked out, and worked fine. The guys in the tent were scared to say the least. At least they had followed the instructions that Bob Downs had given them, in case of attack. They had hunkered down against the dirt floor. Someone said they were so low that they would have had to look-up to see an ant.

There were 87 AK-47 bullet holes through the tent. One of the guys had a spent slug hit him on the upper arm with just enough velocity left (After passing through several cases of cokes and rations) to leave a bright red mark. Also, the skin wasn't broken, and it didn't leave a bruise. I think he still should have qualified for the Purple Heart, but someone said that you have to bleed to get it.

The only real injury to any of the guys was to a Master Sergeant, who was scampering across the dirt floor on his hands and knees, and ran into the tent pole, and busted his head. This guy was suffering from shell-shock, and was on the verge of a nervous breakdown by the time that Bob got there. Afterwards, he was walking around with a death grip on a new 50-cal ammo can, with two bullet holes shot through the box. He had not been hit, not even a scratch. This ended his tour, as he was unable to work after this. It was also reported that eleven friendly troops were killed that night. Needless to say, there were not many volunteers to stay overnight at Moung Soui after this experience.

Moung Soui was finally lost in late June 1969.

I knew Sergeant Smokes personally from the ACA, American Community Association, and the Attache compound. He told me that after he was shot, he played dead. The NVA had kicked him, but he didn't respond. He was extremely upset that the Air Operations personnel in the tent did not engage the enemy. I told him that they had no weapons.

Sergeant Smokes knew in some way, that I had worked at the Moung Soui Air Field, and assumed that I had been in the tent. I immediately told him that my duty had concluded at the runway, and I was back in the Command Post (You didn't want to make Smokes mad. He was a big person. He told me one time the KKK was having a rally in Raleigh, North Carolina, and he went to the rally, and sat on the front row. He didn't say if he had any troops from Fort Bragg with him).

The Sergeant was an acquaintance, and told me that after he was shot, he played dead to keep the enemy from killing him. Without a doubt, he was upset that the AOC personnel did not intervene against the enemy forces.

Regarding the airman in the tent, I do not know if they had received the same military training as I, or not. But even with training, with no weapons, what can you do? (I was one of the Vientiane AIRA Airman (Civilian), not from the Vientiane Air Operations Center).

One of my first duties, outside of command post duty was to train the RLAF. In the light, I began training Laotian officers, and enlisted personnel on how to receive and document information, such as bombs, bullets, rockets, flares, etc. expended from the sites. When the need arose to replenish what was expended, a report would be sent to the United States AID representative.

As always, life was going too good for me. On a particular day, I drove to the RLAF Radio Room, and training site across the street from RLAF Headquarters. While waiting, parked dead still with the left turn signal on, to turn into the facility, a vehicle struck my vehicle in the rear. The hit was hard enough that the bumper had to be replaced, and the rear of the vehicle was damaged. For myself, I suffered a whiplash and hit my knee against the dashboard.

After the accident was resolved, I was taken by the new senior enlisted person, to the U.S. Embassy Clinic for examination. The physician felt around my neck and head, and then I was released. However, later in the evening when I was preparing for bed, I found matted blood from my left knee to my foot. I guess the strike against the dashboard was pretty hard.

The RLAF Commander and I had an outstanding rapport. Of note, one day he and I were talking at his headquarters, and the subject came up about pay, benefits, etc. He told me about a recent event involving a RLAF member. The airman had walked across the MeKong into Thailand. There he stole some chickens for food to feed his family. The General made the airman take the chickens back, and told him to see him (The General), when he needed assistance.

In March 1969, the North Vietnamese released three American prisoners of War. The three were Navy Lieutenant Frischman, Air Force Captain Rumble, and Navy Seaman Heagdal. The North Vietnamese turned over our fellow Americans to officials representing the United States, and were flown to Vientiane aboard an International Control Commission aircraft. I worked till abut 4:00 a.m. the next morning, as all calls made from the Air Attache's Office had to routed through the Command Post.

Lieutenant Frischman had been shot down over North Vietnam, and as too often the case, his arm was broken during the ejection or extraction process. The North Vietnamese doctor's did not follow their oath to treat all patients. Lt. Frischman's wound went unattended for months, which allowed time for a large scab to cover the wound.

For those not familiar, Vietnam, Laos, and Thailand get cold. Snow and ice are not unknown. The Lieutenant's wish for a blanket was filled, but the blanket pulled the scab from the wound. After this, a Vietnamese surgeon removed the Lieutenant's elbow. With American courage and pride, the Lieutenant learned to flex the muscle in his arm. This new found ability allowed the officer to write, smoke a cigarette, etc.

Captain Rumble was a gold mine to his de-briefer. He had memorized an extremely long list of names of individuals he had seen, heard about, or saw their names on prison walls. I worked with Major Rumble later in my career, at Clark Air Base, Republic of the Philippines.

Seaman Headgal's capture was not a combat capture, but yet in a hostile environment. The Seaman had been thrown overboard by his shipmates, and the North Vietnamese found him, and made him a prisoner of war.

Early the same morning, I returned to the Command Post. I was asked to take some money to our American Comrades. They remained at the U.S. Ambassadors residence overnight. As I walked into the Ambassador's drawing room, I observed the three filling out applications for passports.

I asked the Consulate, an acquaintance, why they were filling out the forms? We (the Government) had files on them inches thick! Also, I reminded him that Lt. Frischman was missing one elbow. Well, the three should be glad of one thing, the Consulate Officer was without a doubt far better than his successor.

Early in the 1970s, the duty controller called me, via a HT2 radio, extremely excited. He advised that our most sensitive site was in danger of being over-run, I reported to the Command Post, and contacted the controller at the site, who turned out to be a friend, for an update. He reported that Communist forces had breached the site, and all AOC personnel were in the site's bunker.

After confirmation of the events, I walked to the Red Phone (secure), and contacted the 7th Air Force's Command Center, advised them of the situation, and requested air resources. The 7th Controller told me F-4s and an AC-130 Gunship were being diverted to the besieged site. When the air sorties checked in with us at command post, we gave them a correct radio frequency, and handed them over to the AOC Controller.

After the frightening night was over, our personnel came out of the bunker to a grateful surprise. The area around the bunker, including the concertina wire, was cluttered with dead bodies. Luck in several ways, had been in our personnel's favor, with the most evident being a F-4 short round hit near their bunker. The blast broke off the engagement.

Of note. I recently read an unclassified report by (allegedly), a CIA Station Chief, Skyline, that worked with AIRA at LS-20A, Long Tieng. I may have taken his comments wrong, but it is my belief that he was demeaning the response by the U.S. Air Force on that tragic night.

Let me clue the reader. If Mr. Brisbane, Controller, had not taken the action he did, and in turn, my response, including using the secure phone to call the 7th Air Force for air resources, the night would have ended differently. USAF responded to the Air Attache, or his representative for resources, the CIA was not in the chain of command. I, or the person replacing me, could have been killed that night, while en-route to the command post. To find a replacement would have delayed the response. Thus, in my opinion, the North Vietnamese would have achieved their objective.

During 1972, a Laotian waiter at the American Community Association (ACA) Club approached me while I was eating (The ACA was a benefit provided by the United States Embassy for American employees, who paid a fee to join, Besides the restaurant, the club maintained a commissary for Americans to buy stateside products). He asked me if I could help him enroll into the RLAF Pilot Training Program.

To accomplish this task, I spoke to an employee of the Air Attache, that truly kept a low profile, a professional in every way (Plus had a beautiful wife and/or mistress), about the waiter. It is this individual, who had the authority to authorize entry into the program. The waiter was selected.

Sadly, I never saw the waiter again. I truly hope that after the Communist take over of the entire country in 1973, that he or his family were not harmed, due to the change of government.

As I wrote previously, any sortie entering across the MeKong River, between Thailand and Laos, Vietnam and Laos, Burma and Laos, or Cambodia and Laos, their crew was entitled to hazardous pay. So naturally, any flight deeper into Communist controlled or contested areas, were considered a combat environment. For an authorized air crewmember, such flights, along with contributing circumstances, may be helpful in the crewmember being awarded an Air Medal, and/or other award that would help one in the advancement to a higher pay grade.

Although I was not an authorized air crewmember, I made several flights in-country, as the aircraft's radio operator. On one extremely sensitive flight, the crew consisted of the Air Attache (pilot), the Assistant Air Attache (co-pilot), the crew chief, and myself (radio operator). The destination of our flight was to the extreme Northwestern part of Laos, near the country of Burma. After landing, the pilot, co-pilot, and crew chief had lunch with the Laotian area commander, followed by a private (secret) conversation/meeting. I was loaned a jeep to drive out top the Laotian Army'a Munitions Storage facility. The visit to the facility was at the direction of the Air Attache, to which I wrote, and submitted my report of the storage area.

The most exciting part of the survey flight was the site's approach and departure. The approach was steep, with mountains on both sides of the aircraft, and the runway ran downhill (There were no aborts, once you started rolling, there was no turning back). As far as sights to see, the road to the munitions storage was lined with jungle foliage. However, one came upon an came upon an opening on the left hand side of the road. At the opening was a steep rock stairway, that led up to what looked like a beautiful Buddhist Temple.

On the way back from the site, we stopped at another remote airstrip. At the runway was one of the Raven Forward Air Controllers (FAC). He had on a black cowboy outfit, with a .38 caliber revolver hanging from a holster around his hips. Dodge City in Laos. After arrival at the Command Post, I was given a hand written message from the Air Attache for the FAC. The message told the FAC to cease and desist the wearing of the cowboy outfit, as it was an unfit image for an Air Force officer.

During a visit to our site at Luang Prabang, after departure from Vientiane, the pilot stayed at almost wing level with the MeKong River as far as we could (The enemy was getting better with their artillery fire). My task at Luang Prabang, and the other sites was to brief the controllers on a new Secret Crypto Device to be used when communicating between sites on an un-secure radio frequency.

After landing, the pilot visited with the other aircrew members, and someone drove me to the lane leading to the AOC member's home. The lane was lined with beautiful trees, with long thick branches and leaves, that looked like a canopy covering the lane. Wow! Out of nowhere, an animal was on my shoulder, with its hairy arms around my neck. I jerked the animal from my neck, and threw it against the ground. When I arrived at the house, I told the staff my story. The animal was their pet monkey. Sorry!

The flight to the super-secret LS-20A, to brief procedures for the crypto device was uneventful. We were lucky on this day, as there wasn't any fog in the mountains. While landing, one had to worry about the fog, for at one end of the runway was a natural barrier - a karst. The stone formation ran hundreds of feet high.

After departure, we had been traveling for awhile, when all of the sudden, I saw what seemed to be brownish-white puffs of smoke or clouds, near the aircraft. I tapped the pilot on the shoulder and started to say "What is that?", when we immediately gained altitude, and continued South to Vientiane. The pilot, who later in his career became a four star Air Force General, never did tell me what the puffs were.

Most of the previous pages dealt with my personal participation in the war. Of course, members of the other sites had their own experiences. At Luang Prabang, one of the RAVENS was inbound to the airport, and was in fact, in the airport control zone along with a RLAF helicopter. The RAVEN turned his aircraft ahead of the helicopter. The chopper blades cut the aircraft in half, and the young pilot was killed. The RAVEN had a girlfriend that worked at the U.S. Embassy, Vientiane. I conveyed my grief and support to her after his death.

One of the RAVENS was working in the Long Tieng region, when his aircraft was struck by ground fire. He made a forced landing, and attempted to defend his position with only his aircraft as cover. Both Air America and Continental Air Service helicopter pilots attempted to pick up the officer, but the ground fire was too intense and they had to withdraw.

We had contact with the Search and Rescue on scene Commander, and it is my opinion, that if the Air Force had retained the A-1E Skyraider as the primary rescue aircraft, the pilot would have survived.

At the close of the air warm, our government, with all its wisdom, reassigned all A-1E Skyraider aircraft assigned to the in-country Search and Rescue (SAR), to the government of South Vietnam (For movie goers, you may remember the aircraft that dove out of the sky to drop his ordnance on William Defoe, at his request, in the movie Interceptor).

The A-1E aircraft could loiter for approximately 12 hours, armor plated, and could carry mixed ordnance totaling approximately 36,000 lbs. The replacement aircraft was an A-7 jet aircraft. The aircraft could not loiter, had to go a great distance from the SAR to turn, and could not carry the type and amount of ordnance truly needed for a SAR Mission.

When the North Vietnamese took over South Vietnam in 1975, they took control of the A-1Es, helicopters, and numerous other types of U.S. aircraft. Vietnam became the nation with the largest Air Force in French Indo-China.

Early in my assignment, an officer (and friend of mine) was a RAVEN FAC on his first assignment in-country. His assignment was at the Super Secret Air Base, and he was the lead RAVEN FAC. On a particular day, he was flying a recon mission, when his aircraft developed mechanical problems (At this time in the history of the RAVENS, the site did not have the truly qualified maintenance personnel to assure safe flights). The FAC made an emergency landing in an area designated as a mine field. Search and Rescue picked him up, and returned to his site.

He and the other FACS would not fly anymore sorties until qualified maintenance personnel were assigned or contracted through Air America.

The large framed man that flew to Vientiane with me at our assignments to the project, was killed a few months after he was assigned to one of the Southern AOC sites. On the fateful day, he called his AOC, and reported seeing troop movement on the ground. He further stated that he would descend to see if they were friend or foe. The Golden BB killed him. A lucky shot came through the floor of the aircraft and struck the pilot under his arm. He was the first acquaintance of mine to die in the illegal Laotian air war.

With the U.S. State Department running the war, the rules of engagement were never the same. There was a revision here and there. The day of the AOC Commanders death, the rules for the Commander was to fly with his RLAF students, with the ordnance aboard in question.

This sad day, the Commander flew with live ordnance on board, his aircraft was shot down, and he was killed.

A message from the Embassy stated that his family could not receive benefits, as he was flying an illegal sortie. Soon afterward, I read a message from an Assistant Secretary of State countermanding the order. The military man or woman is but a pawn or puppet to the ruling class.

The FAC that made the emergency landing in a mine field was reassigned to Luang Prabang. He was airborne at the time of an incident involving a bomb that had fallen off a T-28 during the process of taking off. The AOC controller called the center and requested that we send an Emergency Ordnance Disposal team to the site. I went and spoke with the AID person in charge of such a request. By the time AID acted, the FAC had landed and disarmed the weapon himself.

The same FAC was flying in the province where the Chinese were constructing radar artillery operated sites along the road that they were building from China through Laos to Thailand. Suddenly, all hell broke loose from the Chinese gunners. The FAC did some extraordinary flying events to avoid being shot. As he continued to his home station, he discovered a fleet of North Vietnamese Navy vehicles and barges. His findings resulted in heavy battle damage to the North Vietnamese, in their attempt to move logistics to South Vietnam.

At an extreme Southern site, the U.S. had dropped mines around the site to prevent Communist troops from penetrating the outer line of defense. Naturally, the mining did not allow the troops manning the site to leave either. The site had been under siege for a long period of time, which led to many soldiers being killed and critically wounded. RLAF helicopter pilots would not attempt to land at the site to recover the dead and wounded. In this light, a number of the seriously wounded pulled grenade pins and killed themselves. For whatever reasons, one of the oldest pilots assigned to our project flew to the site and landed.j

After he landed RLAF aircrews followed (I remember one day on our C-47, the officer was the co-pilot. We were on approach at an airfield, and he dropped his hands to lower the landing gear. His hands were shaking. I said to myself, "What am I doing here?").

In a previous chapter, I addressed an Emergency Ordnance Disposal (EOD) team. With five sites operational, plus other military activities in the region, an EOD team was always on call at Udorn or Nakhon Phanom, Thailand. One such request for an EOD person involved a Master Sergeant assigned to an EOD team. He had received his retirement orders, and the requested sortie in-country would be his last. It was his last, but not as expected. The site was booby trapped, and he tripped a ground wire.

Not all of those dying were American deaths. After our U.S. pilots trained Laotian pilots they became combat flyers throughout the different regions of the country. One of the pilots was responsible for his own death. He was so determined to destroy the target, he was too low when the ordnance detonated. He was one of many killed in defense of his country.

One day while manning the command post, I received an unfamiliar call sign. I responded, but still did not know who the caller was. I asked one of the officers outside the center, and he said it was a former Long Tieng AOC Commander. He was the lead A-1 pilot for a flight of helicopters and Sky-raiders heading for Son Tay, North Vietnam, to rescue American prisoners at that destination. However due to a flood in the area, American prisoners had been moved.

To continue with this very special event. The rescue team originated at Nakhon Phanom Royal Thai Air Base, Kingdom of Thailand. From Thailand, they flew across Laos, North Vietnam and to the border of China, where the prison was located. Not one American aircraft was lost, except for the one programmed to crash through the prison wall. Prisoners were not found, but U.S. Special Forces left their calling card.

Regarding the Son Tay raid. The Encore Cable Network ran movies in memory of John Wayne recently. A number of dignitaries voiced their praise for Mr. Wayne. One such person was Senator, and former U.S. Prisoner of War, John McCain. Senator McCain told of an after hours party in a California Hotel Bar, where John Wayne was partying with a group of U.S. Special Forces members. McCain recalled

Wayne and the troops address of the famous raid. McCain's words surprised me when he praised the enlisted members that carried out the ground assault. Of note, the prisoner camp was fifty miles from Hanoi. He said that when the POWs heard of the raid, their spirit was lifted.

On the negative note. One day, the Director of Operations called me into his office. He asked me to redo the duty schedule for the Command Post Controllers. I asked why. He replied because he wanted to give one of the controllers some time off. I said no. He started to use some profanity towards me. I saluted him, even though we were supposed to be civilians, and walked out the door.

The situation occurred just before the announcement of promotions. My FAC friend told me that I had been promoted to Master Sergeant (E-7), plus the Air Force Times reported a Billy R. Wilson was promoted to Master Sergeant.

A day or so later, the senior enlisted person called me aside to reprimand me for the conversation with the officer. I made him mad, as I did not cower. I would like to have the money the stripe brought, but the stripe would not have increased my responsibilities. I was already maxed out. I believed in what we were doing until 1972. It was this year, that I knew we were leaving Southeast Asia.

An event that occurred on August 17, 1970, the birth of my son, turned out to be a troublesome day. His mother did not want to go to the United States. The acting U.S. Consulate was not going to allow me to take my son home with me, at my return. With the assistance of the late United States Senator, the honorable John Sherman Cooper, my son came home with me. He has his own residence in London, has two wonderful children, and works for General Electric Train Division.

Early in the morning of December 24, 1972, I received a radio call from a RAVEN. He was departing Vientiane en-route to his working in the LS-20A area. Later in the afternoon, I heard a transmission between him and the Airborne Command and Control Aircraft. So afterwards. The Crash-On-Scene Commander contacted me advising that the RAVEN was down.

Later I learned that the RAVEN had a mid-air collision with an A-7 aircraft. The on-scene authority observed a falling object hit in the tall saw grass, and a trail start at the object. The object was the RAVEN. The A-7 driver ejected, and was captured, but was released during the 1973 Prisoner of War release by the North Vietnamese.

It is my goal, that before my muscles stop functioning, that I will receive funds that will allow me to visit Saigon, Hanoi, and Vientiane. In Hanoi, I will visit the war museum to learn more about the cases I worked while at the Joint Casualty Resolution Center. In Vientiane, I will visit their war museum and speak, if allowed, to the individuals that were responsible for the shoot down region during the war. The Lao are good people.

A number of years past, I believe I read in Time Magazine, that the Laotian government had erected a memorial to the United States, for its work in the Kingdom. Yes, our country dropped a lot of ordnance in Laos. Through the hard work of the U.S. State Department, the Central Intelligence AID, and the Department of Defense, Laos was brought from a backward nation, without most benefits that a civilized nation enjoys, to a nation with an airline, television, radio, up-to-date airport, hospitals, telephones, etc. We did good, not outstanding.

Regarding the war in South Vietnam, and the United States Department of Veteran Affairs (DOVA). Today, the DOVA does not recognize Department of Defense member's service in the Kingdom of Laos, pertaining to disability claims. As a matter of history and fact, South Vietnam would have been over taken long before 1975, and the number of American deaths and wounded greatly increased, had it not been for the United States Departments of Government identified.

Wurtsmith Air Force Base, Michigan

Before I relate events at Wurtsmith Air Force Base, Oscoda, Michigan, I'll explain how I received the assignment. As you know from the Royal Kingdom of Laos chapter, I fathered a son, out of wedlock, while in-country.

Everyone in AIRA knew, including myself, that I had stayed too long in Laos. I did give another assignment a thought, but it was turned down. So, I volunteered for another assignment in Southeast Asia. I received notification of an assignment to U-Tapao Royal Thai Air Base, Kingdom of Thailand.

My son's mother did not want to come to the United States with me and our son (I went to Laotian Court to be granted full custody of our son).The U-Tapao assignment would have been perfect, had it not been for the deteriorating political system in Laos, and withdrawal of funding for Southeast Asia by Congress. The full U.S. Congress knew about the illegal war in Laos at that point. I spoke with Colonel Curry, the Air Attache, and wrote Air Force personnel, asking for my assignment to be to U-Tapao. With Colonel Curry's assistance, the assignment was cancelled, and I received a new assignment to Wurtsmith Air Force Base, Oscoda, Michigan. A Strategic Air Command Base.

You may recall that my Mother was deceased and I was divorced. So, a single father with a 2 year, 4 month old son, it would pose a problem for me to remain in the United States Air Force. The solution for my

Mother was resolved, as I had two Aunts in Detroit, that were really close to me. My Aunt Alpha wrote that she would hire a maid to take care of my son, while I remained in the Air Force, or assumed control of her business and rental property.

My Aunt Alpha did not work out. I learned that she was dishonest, and had failed to keep her promise to care for my son. My friend that I served with in Florida and Korea, lived in Livonia, Michigan along with his wife. They cared for my son for a few months, after I took him from my crooked Aunt's home. Finally, my young Aunt offered to care for my son for pay. So, for most of my son's life, he was under the supervision of my younger Aunt.

Wurtsmith was an alternate base. I had requested an assignment at Selfridge Air National Guard Base, Michigan. The base was located North-Northeast of Detroit. The base was a National Guard base, therefore, the air operations personnel were civilians.

Wurtsmith was a good choice, as it was several hundred miles almost due North of Detroit (Highways North of Detroit were excellent). A plus factor for Wurtsmith was Alpena, Michigan. Since David came to the United States as a Lao immigrant, I had to go before a Federal Court and Federal Judge to make his birth legal, and award him his American citizenship.

The acting U.S. Consulate, In Vientiane, denied my son's birth right, as the son of an American citizen, and made him enter the United States as a Lao immigrant. To correct the Consulate's bias was expensive, and time consuming, but in the end, the stress and money were worth U.S. citizenship.

Mother nature was watching over me (I believe we have a predetermined fate at birth, but we have to make it happen. One cannot be on welfare, smoke, drink alcohol, etc.). My operations officer, operations staff, base commander, peers, and the civilians that I worked with were real human beings, and did everything possible for me. The term "Officer and Gentlemen" truly applied to the Base Commander, and the Officers of Base Operations.

As I wrote previously, my son's mother did not want to come to the United States, but I still kept aware of her status, through our former American neighbor and his Thai wife (He was the civilian supervisor of the Army's Communication Center). I learned that she had cut her wrist. I requested an emergency leave, which was granted. In fact, the Base Commander authorized the expenditure of travel funds on my behalf.

Knowing the political environment at the U.S. Embassy, and the Air Attache Office because of my actions against the U.S. Consulate Officer. I went to the Lao Embassy, in Bangkok, immediately after I arrived in Thailand. The consulate staff asked the purpose for the visa. I explained, and the visa was issued.

I took Thai Airways to Laos, and found my son's mother. She was ill, besides her wrist being cut. To my knowledge, the best medical facility was the Embassy's Clinic, so I visited the new U.S. Consulate seeking paid permission to take my lady friend for tests. We worked out the medical problems, and I gave my son's mother $1500.00 to help her out, even though she now had a Marine Embassy Guard as her boyfriend. The lady Consulate was an understanding person.

Sure enough, one day I was out at a club near the airport, frequented by the spooks, Air America, Continental, Mr. Civilians, and others, when in walked the senior enlisted person from the Air Attache's Office. I told him that I had a Lao Tourist Visa, and that I would stay until resolution of my lady friends troubles. She married the Marine.

Through the expert management of Base Operations, the competent military, and civilian work force, my duties at Wurtsmith were not complicated. I no longer worked 12 to 14 days for weeks at a time. In fact, because of the outstanding working environment, I had a part time job making pizza in the Base Exchange's Pizza Pub, after my duty hours, and on weekends. I had to pay off the debt incurred by bringing my son to the United States.

The Base Operations Officer had been a KC-135 refueling pilot in the Vietnam War, and knew of the command post that I used to be in charge of. We could talk about the war and other subjects like 2 people, rather than officer and enlisted person. In fact, I was invited to the officers home for meals, and good conversation. The base, and my supervisors were outstanding.

The next step is debatable. My son was now with my mother's younger sister. Her daughter had a son, my son's age. My son was enrolled in a Catholic school. The school may have created conflict for my son. Honesty and goodness was taught at school, and the exact opposite was the norm at my Aunt's home (I learned this after the fact).

I learned of a Joint U.S. Military organization being established, whose mission was to resolve the status of U.S. Missing in Action from the Vietnam War. Since I was in some cases, the last person to speak with search and rescue or other units, involved in a shoot-down or rescue, I volunteered for the Joint Casualty Resolution Center.

At the receipt of my orders, the staff at Wurtsmith bid me farewell, and the best of luck. Without a doubt, in my entire military career, the officers, overall, at Wurtsmith were the best that I ever served. My assignment at Wurtsmith was less than 9 months.

My son was too young to understand, but my Aunt knew about my deep convictions regarding the United States' involvement in the Southeast Asian War. I was wrong, my son didn't understand. He has ill feelings against me to this date.

Joint Casuality Resolution Center (Jcrc)

September 1973, approximately nine months since departing the Kingdom of Laos, I was back, but on the other side of the Mekong River in Thailand. The base was Nakhon Phanom Royal Thai Air Base, Kingdom of Thailand. The assignment was to the Joint Casualty Resolution Center (JCRC).

The center, allegedly, was established to resolve the status of U.S. Missing in Action (MIA), from the Vietnam War era. The task would be through physical search of all sites known to be the shoot down location, and/or the last known point of contact. Another method would be the administrative review of classified, and un-classified documents obtained from foreign governments, paid informants, and former military members, who were associated with the member prior to his/her disappearance. Allegedly, no stone would go unturned.

In my opinion, the 1973-1974 JCRC was established as a political appeasement to the MIA's next of kin, continued intelligence scrutiny of Vietnam Communists, and an avenue for Army and Marines officers to get promoted.

The true resolution of the missing occurred during the Clinton Administration. To this end, I do not know if my inputs were beneficial or not. I wrote to Mr. Tony Lake, and the U.S. State Department about the MIA in the Kingdom of Laos. I provided names of royals, and others in the Kingdom that could assist in the recovery of missing Americans. Needless to say, I never received a response, but action was taken, as a number of remains have been recovered from Laos. Vietnam remains were recovered as well.

JCRC was a true eye-opener. I had worked with special forces, and artillery advisors in Laos, but at this assignment, it was a true joint assignment. At least in Laos, service personnel were there to fight an illegal war, but JCRC was about getting promoted.

My immediate supervisor was an Air Force Major. He had previously been attached to the U.S. Marine Corps. The purpose of the assignment was for the Air Force to become familiar with the worthless Harrier aircraft through the Major. So he became an Air Force officer flying a Harrier (The Major encountered a hard landing while piloting the Harrier).

The Current Operations Division was under the leadership of a Marine Lieutenant Colonel. The Lt. Colonel was a hard core Marine.

The Vice Commander of the organization was an Air Force Colonel (My friend the RAVEN FAC told me that he had been offered the position as Vice Commander, but turned it down. At the time of my telephone call seeking advise about the organization, he was the commander of C-130 Hurricane Hunter Squadron in Mississippi. A wise friend).

The Commander of the Joint Casualty Resolution Center was an Army One Star General. He wanted promotion, in my opinion, regardless of the number of Americans killed to dig up bones (His replacement was an Officer and a Gentleman, not a killer of men).

The year of assignment was September 1973. The North Vietnamese and Pathet Lao had already taken over the entire country of Laos. The King was removed from his throne. In South Vietnam, the people, and the military were awaiting the onslaught of the North Vietnamese. South Vietnam was over-run in 1975.

The Marine Lt. Colonel acted like the war was still raging, and Communist Forces would over-run the base. However, his true work days would not have washed in the U.S. Air Force. General (Sundown) Wilson would have recommended his loss of command. His habit of participating in sporting events, and then expecting an enlisted person to hold his hand in the evenings and on weekends, would have expedited his departure as a commander. Air Force personnel work basically without officer supervision. The officer signs his name.

I can still recall a senior Air Force Officer that told me during my first years at Homestead, "If you can't do your job, Monday through Friday, 8:00 a.m. - 5:00 p.m., then you're not doing your job." His words did not mean during alert periods, or actual war. The non-administrative airman worked until the aircraft was OR (operational ready), munitions up-loaded or down-loaded. Other career fields, such as the medical corps, had personnel at the ready to care for any emergency.

Since I did not drink coffee, make coffee, nor was I a play time military hawk. I did not fit in with Lt. Colonels view of his military. I was reassigned to the true meat of the organization JCRC'S Intelligence Section. The section's senior enlisted person was a true soldier (I spoke to him a year or so later, when he was at Fort Devens, MA. I was at Pease Air Force Base, New Hampshire, and I was looking for a tent to sign out. The tent was going to be for a MASH party, the passenger service section was going to hold).

In the intelligence section, we reviewed Top Secret Prisoner of War Debriefs, screened classified reports from foreign governments aligned with the United States, read paid informers filings, studied Defense Intelligence Agency (DIA) communications, were engrossed by the CIA's documents, and were enlightened by shoot-down/ground search evidence summaries. Our efforts were to change all MIA status to "DECEASED, BODY NOT RECOVERED'/"DECEASED, BODY NOT RECOVERABLE.'

At first, I attempted to reside on base, in the barracks provided by the command. However, assigned to the billets, were individuals, whom I may say, did not meet the standards of the United States Air Force. U.S. Special Forces shared our compound. You never knew when you would have hot water to take a shower. Equally important, I would not eat in the NCO Club, or the mess hall (Too many people. I do not like crowds).

Luck was with me again. One of the Army enlisted persons that I worked with was married to a Thai woman, and between them had a couple of children. He had a pick-up truck with a metal canopy, and home in the town of Nakhon Phanom. I struck a deal with him to ride, to and from town, to the base each day. Also, I rented a Western style house, and hired a live in maid. The maid was a massage specialist.

The house was two story. An army specialist, his Vietnamese wife, and their children lived above my residence. The next house over was a Command First Sergeant, his Thai wife, and children. The western homes were owned by a Vietnamese woman.

Ho Chi Minh was a special person in the city of Nakhon Phanom, and the province. The town square was named Ho Chi Minh. Minh used to frequent Nakhon Phanom before the U.S. attacked North Vietnam.

Nakhon Phamon was not unlike many towns/cities in Thailand. A number of Americans from the military, civil service, Air America, and other organizations retired in-country. One American, married to a Vietnamese woman, had a bar and restaurant where many of us ate. The food was good, and the clients limited.

Late 1973 or early 1974, I went to Vientiane, Laos on temporary duty (TDY). The purpose of the trip was to recover MIA documents from the U.S. Embassy's Consulate Section. JCRC was missing 13 Top Secret documents.

Wow! What a change. I flew into Vientiane, via an Air America aircraft. I hailed a taxi for the ride from the airport to where I would stay in Vientiane. En-route, we passed the old French School that I wrote about previously. The school building, and compound appeared to be in use. One could see row after row of double bunk beds. The courtyard was clean. I suspected the communist forces were using the school as a barrack.

Instead, at one of the hotels where I'm sure government agents would be located, I decided to rent a room in Dong Phalane (The red light district). The district was where my girlfriend, son, and I lived prior to my son and I returning home to the United States.

Boy was I surprised at what I observed that evening. I never saw once during my previous four years in Vientiane, the Laotian Army in the same capacity. Yes, when Communist forces were acting up in-country, there were road blocks and curfews. The surprise was seeing columns of Communist troops, in their brand new Chinese uniforms, and ever typical Chinese cap, patrolling the streets, armed with their AK-47s. The city was in the control of the Communist rulers for sure.

I rented an apartment from my former home owner, but I never stayed in the room. I stayed overnight with a lady friend of my son's mother, and of course, my friend. My son's mother and husband had been transferred to the Bangkok Embassy. He was a U.S. Marine Embassy Guard.

The TDY turned out to be a gold mine of classified documents. In fact, I found 13 Top Secret documents that belonged to JCRC (Given out prior to the assigned senior enlisted person, I addressed). I collected enough classified documents to till a large white burlap bag. The documents collected provided me, and other intelligence personnel with material that assisted in the resolution of a number of MIA cases. There could have been more resolved had it not been for certain services not wanting to reclassify their MIAs.

At last it was time to return to Thailand. A U.S. Embassy driver, and a guard (I suppose he was a guard) drove me to the Air America's Security Chief's Office. At Air America, I would await the plane that would fly me, and the recovered documents back to Nakhon Phanom.

As I walked into the chief's office, I was stunned. What stunned me was an extremely large black and white photograph of Che Guevara. There was Che dead, and on a stretcher. I asked where he got the photo. He replied, "I took it." He had been part of the U.S. Special Forces Teams that tracked down Che and killed him. A truly interesting day.

My arrival back at JCRC was a blessing for the Senior Non-Commissioned Officer. He now had his missing thirteen documents, plus the other material that I recovered. So for the next few days, this NCO had the task of documenting, and storing what was recovered. This time whenever you withdrew a document for review, you had to sign for the document. Classified documents were now controlled.

The U.S. governments policy in Laos was whenever an aircrew was shot down, or troops ambushed, etc., as soon as the site became secure enough to send in a recovery team, it was done. A number of these searches recovered information that allowed us to resolve cases. For example, a F-105 had crashed into a karst, killing the pilot, and destroying the aircraft. A team recovered parts of the aircraft with serial, and part numbers, plus bits and pieces of his body (Fibula and others), and flight suit. I spent several days on this project, and in the end, I made a folder, proving through the items recovered, it was in fact, the body of the F-105 pilot. The U.S. Air Force agreed, and his status was changed to "Deceased, Body Recovered."

Returning back to the Vientiane TDY, I learned two Air America dependents were in Vientiane seeking permission from the Communists, for permission to physically visit the crash site of their husbands. A number of Air America pilots were shot down and killed while others were rescued. A lady friend of mine, her father's aircraft was shot down. His remains were quickly recovered.

Wow! To my pleasant surprise, I found a couple of documents regarding the pilot's bodies. A search team had recovered the bodies, taken them to JCRC'S laboratory, and positively identified. The lab had sent out a message telling our organization to notify the next of kin to pick-up the remains. We failed to notify the next of kin.

After finding the information, and knowing about the wives, I spoke with my boss, another Air Force Major. He failed to grasp the situation. I next went to an Army Lt. Colonel, and repeated the story of evidence. Again, no answer. Finally, I went past the Army Master Sergeant logging individuals into see the General and Colonel, and knocked on the Vice Commander's door. The Colonel asked me what I wanted. Based on my report, he told the proper authorities to investigate the incident. The answer came back, it wasn't our organization's responsibility.

Well once again, I stuck my ass out. I called an American lady friend and told her the history of the remains. She told the wives of the MIA husbands. The wives in turn, went to the Embassy and raised hell. Allegedly, one wife called the command and told them that I better not be in trouble, as she was not without political influence. Since the information I released was not classified, I didn't receive any punishment. Yes, JCRC was embarrassed and angry.

Again regarding documents recovered, I came across photographs of Americans being captured by civilians. Dog tags, parts of aircraft, and other material taken from American military personnel. The source of the intelligence was unknown. The photographs were from the North Vietnamese War Museum in Hanoi. Based on this find, I wrote a "TALKING PAPER" suggesting further interest in the Hanoi museum. I heard nothing back.

In 1993, our government disclosed to the American people of finding information at Hanoi's War Museum, which were used to re-open cases of the missing. This could have been the same information I submitted in 1973/1974.

A sad, terrible event for JCRC personnel. The command put together a team for the recovery of U.S. remains in Bien Hoa Province, South Vietnam. When the team arrived at the village near the site, the village leader allegedly told the project leader, that the site was under six to eight inches of water. But more important, the chief would not allow his villagers to go to the site because it was booby trapped, and allegedly, the Viet Cong or other Communist had set up an ambush for when the team arrived. There were always booby traps, and that was why an Emergency Disposal Team was part of the recovery teams.

The project leader of the recovery team decided not to proceed with the recovery effort. The Army Captain that was the team leader, had been awarded the Army Silver Star for his previous actions during the Vietnam War. Allegedly he was told, that should his team take ground fire or any other aggressive acts, he should stand up and identify himself as an American.

The Captain and his team proceeded to board the Vietnamese helicopters, and fly to the site. Allegedly when the third chopper was near the ground, the enemy opened fire. The Captain was killed following his orders. Other members of the team were wounded. Had it not been for the brave Vietnamese pilots flying the choppers, all team members could have been killed.

The reason I am so familiar with the incident, is that I was one of the individuals tasked to debrief the team members. To the man, the team said the recovery mission was a going away gift for the departing General to brief at the Pentagon.

The period of time at JCRC, I never deployed with a recovery team into Cambodia, Laos, or South Vietnam. However, the Army person that I rode to and from work with, did in fact go on an intelligence document recovery trip. A former employee of the CIA, a Thai FAG that I knew from Laos, approached me one day in Nakhon Phanom. He told me that he had notes and papers from the Communist Headquarters in Northern Laos.

Just about every year, our forces would drive the Communists out of certain areas. Then in the wet season, the Communist would re-take the land. However, the last great push that I remember, our forces went all the way to Sam Nuea Province (Headquarters for the Pathet Lao). A great victory for the Laotian Government and the Central Intelligence Agency.

I briefed command on my plans to collect the documents and obtained their approval, which allowed us to use a government truck. The Army Sergeant drove the truck.

The village where the Thai lived was called Mukdahan,Thailand. Across the Mekong River from Mukdahan was Savannakhet, the largest Laotian city in the province. The Air Attache had an Air Operations Center at this location.

Continuing South from Mukdahan, one would reach a U.S. Aiar Base located at Ubon, Thailand. The base was named Ubon Royal Thai Air Base. Allegedly, Ubon had encountered some hostile activities over the period of the base's existence. The answer to why was quite simple. Across the Mekong from Ubon was Pakse, Laos.

Pakse was the largest city in this province. The Air Attache had an Air Operations Center in Pakse, due to the Communist activity at Saravan and Attapu. For the history buffs, Saravan was located on the Ho Chi Minh travel, and a constant target for U.S. Special Forces from South Vietnam.

En-route to the village, we had to go through contested and Communist controlled land areas. We were stopped at several checkpoints, but I suppose being in a U.S. Government vehicle and military identification cars was all the authority that the Thai Police and soldiers required to allow us to proceed.

I do not recall the Thai nationals name, but his CIA call sign was "Super Stud." Super Stud had been present when the CIA and Laotian achieved their great victory over Communist forces at Sam Nuea.

Sam Nuea was the main headquarters region for North Vietnam and Pathet Lao Forces in Laos. Due to the cave system, Sam Nuea was also a major logistics center. The victory reaped a bounty of extremely valuable classified Communist documents, equipment, weapons, and other items that an exiled government would have in their war of independence. More important, in my opinion, was the confirmation of Chinese and Chinese government participation in the Laotian War. He turned over papers to us, which in turn, we turned over to command. We, the soldier and I, collected what money we had on our person, and gave it to Super Stud. I apologized that we did not have more money, but I would try to get more. I failed.

Previous history of Super Stud. At different sites in Laos, the agency had American and indigenous personnel assigned normally at larger sites. At the smaller sites, the indigenous was more likely to be assigned without an agency person (The reason being, to keep the American agent from being captured).

For the smaller site, the Pathet Lao, North Vietnamese would place forces around three sides of the sites. They would use a loud speaker to inform the site that if they laid down their weapons, they were free to leave. This happened to Super Stud. He escaped such a site, and made his way through the jungle to friendly territory, and then re-joined with the agency.

I truly hope that Super Stud was terminated for his actions with the Sergeant and myself.

Unprofessional, the Laotian officers were known at the end of the day to fly a large, more secure site and leave only enlisted men, and the agencies indigenous person at the site.

Regarding Americans assigned to non-AIRA sites. A strange situation occurred one evening. An agency person was stranded at a site for whatever reason. To protect the case officer, the United States Air Force's Candlestick orbited the site all evening. The Candlestick kept the site illuminated like daylight. The agency person survived an overnighter.

One day the new Vice Commander asked me to come to his office (The new Vice Commander was a former Special Operations Group person). He told me of a reporter in Saigon, speaking to the press regarding a U.S. Radar/TACAN site over-run by Communist Forces in Laos. He knew of my history in Laos, and asked me to write a report. I complied.

The site in question was the 6th on the Air Attache's Command Post radio net. Allegedly, senior officials atop the mountain informed command that Communist Forces were amassing at the base of the mountains, and asked to be withdrawn.

Allegedly, the U.S. Embassy did not believe the climb and assault could be made. The project personnel and indigenous secured themselves in an on-site bunker. Thirteen individuals were killed that evening. One Air Force person was recently awarded the Congressional Medal of Honor for his deeds. His family received the medal, as he was killed.

Not all those assigned were killed. A number of airman survived. I served under one of the rescued. He was the Pease Air Force Base Wing Commander.

Air strikes were launched from Nakhon Phanom to destroy the site. The site was not re-built, but replaced by an aircraft configured to replace the air traffic control functions.

In 1990, while working in the Admissions Section at the Louisville Veterans Administration Hospital, I met on of the enlisted radar controllers that had been assigned to the site. He was discharged from the Air Force with a diagnosis of Post Traumatic Disorder.

One day, while reading Top Secret Documents (since declassified are now public knowledge), I learned that the alleged attack on the U.S. Turner Joy, in the Gulf of Tonkin, was a fabricated story (You may recall that President Johnson used the Tonkin incident to increase the number of U.S. troops in South Vietnam). In fact, the U.S. Navy already had targets selected in North Vietnam to strike, awaiting the order from Washington. That day turned out to be a heartbreaking day. Here I was, a dumb Kentucky man that believed his government.

One day while we were reading classified documents and completing forms for computer input, a hard stripe Army Sergeant asked me the following question. "Would I change coordinates of shoot-downs in Laos to Vietnamese coordinates?" I said No. He then replied, "I didn't think you would."

The air base had another special tenant, the unit was a monitoring, and information collecting agency. What the general public does not know is that our government dropped sensors, and other devices on the Ho Chi Minh Trail that could distinguish the difference between genders. One could go on and on about the accomplishments of the U.S. Military, and other sensitive agencies of the U.S. Government. It was not the military and CIA that caused the United States to withdraw from Southeast Asia, but individual politicians with agendas, other than the security and prosperity of the United States. History hasn't changed from the Vietnam era. A mentally imbalanced President of the United States ordered a Religious Crusade on the sovereign nation of Iraq.

The months I spent with JCRC were not wasted. I learned to much regarding the struggles, self sacrifices, courage, honor, and most of all, the beliefs by the American military man/woman regarding our great nation.

Of course, anytime you have politics in a military event, an occurrence happens. For example, I wrote about the joy by the American Prisoners of War (POW) to learn that an unsuccessful POW rescue had been made on the Son Tay Prison 23 miles from Hanoi. From reading the Top Secret Debriefs, I know of an incident that made them happier.

As was the practice of the North Vietnamese to allow the POW yard time (I don't know the intervals). On this usual, hot, muggy day, the POWs were in the yard. Someone spotted a small dark object on the horizon. Soon the horizon was increasing in size. The object was a F-111 Fighter/Bomber.

Located extremely close to the prison was a large communications tower. This tower was the target of the F-111. Ordnance released. The tower was hit. Shrapnel and debris filled the air. The North Vietnamese guards told the prisoners to return to the prisons. Many stood amongst the shrapnel and debris, yelling in favor to the top of their lungs. The U.S. did something.

An officer had been in the prison for awhile, and by watching, devised an escape plan that would make the screenwriters of the Great Escape movie with Steve McQueen and James Garner proud.

The plan called for the officer to climb into the ceiling of the prison and make his way across the cells until he reached the outside. The escape was for the evening hours, naturally. Once outside the prison, he would walk or jump into the river. The river would, in-turn, take him out to the gulf, where he could be picked up by an American warship.

Wait, another officer wanted to go with planner. Sadly to report, the other officer was truly not in the same physical or mental condition as the planner for the escape.

The two made it into the water. The weaker officer became disoriented and started flaying in the water. The planner had to rescue the officer. They discovered an enclave in the river's bank, and they hid there for the rest of the night.

At daylight, the weaker of the two men jumped up, started yelling, and running back toward the prison camp. They were both captured.

The planner was not so lucky. The Cuban officer assigned to the North Vietnamese prison system, beat the officer to death with a fan belt. His nickname was Fidel (I hope someone in our government took it upon themselves to see that Fidel was terminated with extreme prejudice. Individuals like George W. Bush and Richard Cheney should be brought before an international court for Crimes Against Humanity).

There was a Marine Corp Major and Navy Lieutenant Commander, who were the hosts of an anti - U.S. radio program transmitted in the prison camp, and over the airways. Due to their collaboration, these individuals were given freedoms, such as walks outside the walls of the prison.

The cited individuals became friends with Jane Fonda and her husband, which may have influenced the military's refusal to Court Martial them.

Then an example of military's two standards. An enlisted Marine had trouble living up to Marine standards, and was too often in a jam with his senior enlisted officer - stateside. He received orders to transfer to South Vietnam.

His failures did not cease aboard the troop ship taking the Marines to Vietnam. He ended up in the ship's Brig for some infraction.

Ashore in Vietnam, he was assigned as a Marine driver. While driving through the Vietnamese countryside, he was captured, and taken to North Vietnam.

In North Vietnam, he worked around the American POWs, helping them in any way he could. Finally disillusioned, he wrote a note to a

Westerner and that individual was instrumental in his release from the North Vietnamese.

Upon return to the United States, he came before a Court Martial board and was found guilty. It's just who you know.

At JCRC, we would have frequent government sponsored individuals, such as the wives, family members of the MIAs, politicians, and the news media, etc. The command would provide a tour, maybe a repelling exercise from a helicopter, or some other demonstration of the power of the U.S. military.

The Vice Commander called me in, and told me to go set up transportation with Nakhon Phanom's USAF Wing Commander for the wife of a MIA, to catch up with the rest of her group, already in Bangkok. It appears the lady met an Australian in Bangkok, enjoyed herself, and had come up-country alone. I received assistance from the Wing Commander and the lady was on her way.

One last, sad but true story. In the North Vietnamese prison, if a North Vietnamese, Cuban Russian, Chinese, North Korean, or any other government official walked into a prisoners room, he was to get up and bow. The Major never bowed. Finally, on the day of his death, an attendant could use a surgical instrument on his body sores without any pain. He was oblivious to pain. The why, of why the Cuban Fidel had beat him so many times with the fan belt, because he no longer felt pain.

Without a doubt, what I have written, if anyone bothers to read my book, will go to the shelf as a book read. However, it is time for true Americans to rid this country of Zionist. Jews and Old Testament Christians are destroying the United States of America, and the elected President of that country.

Regardless of the legal or illegal reason for war, the military man/woman accomplishes the task set forth. However in the future, we seek

Americans, not hyphenated Americans, for the Congress of the United States will assure that military deaths and injuries were not in vain. The person/persons, such as former President Bush & Vice President Cheney, met the fate imposed by the U.S. Constitution for the act of TREASON.

My head and body were messed up from duty in Laos, but reading day to day about Americans being shot in the back of the head, dropped on punji sticks, beaten with fan belts, etc., I had had enough. I wrote the Commander asking that I be reassigned or discharged, the assignment was overwhelming. I received orders to Pease Air Force Base, New Hampshire.

Pease Air Force Base

The assignment at Pease Air Force Base, Portsmouth, New Hampshire was extremely enlightening and beneficial. The wing commander, as a junior officer, had been at the Radar/TACAN Site over-run a few months prior to my arrival in Laos. When we came to base operations for a visit or meet a VIP, we could and did speak of the illegal war in the former French Indo-China.

I hadn't been at Pease long, when memory of events and lack of action at the JCRC would not let my mind rest. So, as the psych doctor said "don't hold in your thoughts, lay them out". I did just that, I wrote the honorable, now deceased, Senator John Tower of Texas, who at the time I believe, was Chairman of the Senate's Armed Service Committee. The senator or his staff acknowledged the letter and informed me the letter had been forwarded to the Pentagon.

Several months later, I received notification that my presence had been requested before a Pentagon Board investigating the Joint Casualty Resolution Center. Base Headquarters issued Temporary Travel Orders funded by the air base.

Being naïve, I truly believed we, members at the investigating board, were going to address the U.S. Missing In Action question.

I flew in to Washington, D.C., the evening before the day of inquiry and spent the evening in a four star hotel. The next morning I took a taxi to the Pentagon. (Wow! What a building).

Walking in the entrance door of the Pentagon, I was met by a Navy Lieutenant Commander who was my guide to the board room. Prior to sitting down at the table, a officer approached me and asked if I needed legal council. I replied no. I had no reason for legal support.

So, into the room of military officers sitting at a giant hardwood table with tape recorder and a court stenographer. So help me. The first question asked, in an official capacity, was "Was the Vice Commander of JCRC sleeping with his American Secretary?". (An Air Force Colonel held the position as Vice Commander. An Army General Kingston was the commander). The question pissed me off but I remained cool.

I told the questioner I did not know. The reason could have been that I didn't reside in the barracks. After a short period at the center, I rented a western style house from a Vietnamese woman. I asked a massage girl to move in with me and be my maid. I paid her a monthly salary and bought her items as she needed them.

The reason I could reside off base was that one of the Army Sergeants that worked with me had a Thai wife and children. He had a Thai style home in the city of Nakhon Phanom, and a pick-up truck with a Thai style canopy over the truck's bed. Besides myself, an Army Specialist shared the transportation. He had a Vietnamese wife and children.

I said to myself, there are approximately three thousand U.S. Military personnel in Southeast Asia unaccounted for and the board was worried who the Colonel was sleeping with.

Personal questions were not just about the Vice Commander but my own personal life. A questioner asked me about the Army Specialist, I shared the transportation and apartment with. I told the officer that the army specialist, his wife, and children lived above my section of the two story house that we rented. Each shared the monthly rent payment. As far as being concerned about the specialist, I didn't give a shit. I was hoping that he and his wife would not have the same problems I did when I tried to take my son back to the United States.

An air officer would have never asked such a question. However, when you serve at a joint assignment with the Army and Marines, you quickly learn of their silliness and abuse of manpower and governmental resources. More important, Army and Marine officers will get you killed to get promoted and/or outstanding Officer's Proficiency Report.

After the questioning was over, I returned to Pease. I learned later, the board wasn't interested in the Missing In Action. Their questions were to ascertain if the Joint Casualty Resolution Center was justified in being awarded the Army's Outstanding Unit Award. Some months later, I received orders that awarded me the Army's Outstanding Unit Award.

One day in Base Operations, the chief of Air Operations, a Lieutenant Colonel asked me to come into his office. He asked me why I didn't test for Master Sergeant. I told him the stripe didn't matter. He replied, you are doing the job, so why not take the test. I did, and I was promoted in the next promotion cycle. (I believe for the second time as identified herein).

With the new stripe and the personal rapport I had with the Wing Commander, Base Commander, Chief of Operations and section heads of flying organizations, I was able to save the United States and Pease herself allocated funds. I used the information I learned from the Master Sergeant at Malmstrom Air Force Base, Montana to initiate a new distribution and expenditure of funds, pertaining to aircrew flight publications.

I proposed a suggestion that would allow base F-111 sorties the ability of not shutting down their engines and filing a new flight plan when some aspect of their original flight plan became void.

My suggestion entailed the wing providing the Boston Air Routing Traffic Control with numbered canned flight plans that would cover all situations. This suggestion would save fuel, time, effort and be down right more professional. The proposal was approved.

On the human resources side of base operations, one of the airman working for me had been an Army Medic in Vietnam. He had informed personnel that he did not want the responsibility for another person's life. Air Operations was the wrong profession. I asked him if he would like to transfer out of base operations, he agreed.

I wrote the squadron commander, the base personnel officer, plus the airman had the right AQU scores to cross train. We were able to transfer him back into the medical career field, but as an administrative person instead of a hands on medic. His previous medical experience gave him an advantage over other trainees in his career field for advancement.

The personal side at Pease was not bad, but not good either. I had an affair with a legally separated Korean Woman. I drank every now and then. The drinking showed the lack of wisdom on my part due to my inability to control alcohol.

At Base Operations, the Non-Commissioned Officer in Charge of Passenger Service, was a Technical Sergeant. Over the months, she and I became really close friends. No, no sexual contact, just friends. She had a little blue Volkswagen which we drove a number of times in the mountains of New Hampshire and surrounding states. We crawled through a cave, rode a tourist train, visited an Indian site, etc. With her friendship, my tour passed fast.

A small world. While working in the Kingdom Saudi Arabia, after I retired, I went to the Philippines on vacation (my new wife was Filipino). Who do you think I met at the Military Airlift's Passenger Terminal? None other than my air force lady friend from Pease. She asked me what I was doing since retirement. I told her I was in Saudi Arabia's training Royal Saudi Air Force Warrant Officers. She said she wasn't surprised.

With the U.S. Air Force scheduled to fly Vietnamese babies out of Vietnam, a request for air traffic assistance in the territory of Guam arose. I volunteered. The air traffic was quite heavy but the effort to make the children free from communism was worth whatever extra effort, if any, was exerted.

Not all went well at Guam. An American naval freighter (the Mayaquez) was attacked and hijacked by Cambodians. A number of Americans from Nakhon Phanom and Marines were killed due to the incompetence of the U.S. State Department. Also, command wanted to send the B-52 flight plans over the ICAO, as per international agreement with the United Nations. I reminded leadership of what I had learned in Thailand about the enemy receiving the flight information from the required ICAO transmissions. Another mode was used to prevent disclosure.

I returned to Pease knowing I had done what the Strategic Air Command demanded - my job.

President Carter visited Pease and the Portsmouth area. With the Base Operations officer at his home in Maine, I was the Base Operations officer for that important day.

Not too long after returning from Guam, I received orders for transfer to Clark Air Base, Republic of the Philippines.

No history about Pease Air Force Base would be complete without writing about Sam the Taxi Driver.

Since Pease was located near lobster waters, transient aircrews would load up with lobster and other fish dishes, while their aircraft were being serviced and/or clearing U.S. Customs. The crews would arrange with Sam from their departure point or while en-route through the base operations dispatcher their seafood orders. Sam would have the order on ice awaiting the aircrews.

Like the Passenger Service Supervisor, I considered Sam a friend. Ho took me where I wanted to go in his taxi. He invited me to his home. He was a good person.

Sam had just brought me home from a night out, when I started having sharp pains in my side. I went to the hospital emergency room. The doctors removed my appendix later in the evening.

As at Wurtsmith, the officers, enlisted and civilians at Pease were extremely nice people. I was immature a couple of times. However, on my own behalf, American dead and wounded weighed heavy on my mind and still do.

Clark Air Base, Republic Of The Philippines

I wasn't sure what to expect at Clark Air Base. The country of the Philippines had once been a territory of the United State. (Results of our war with Spain). The Philippines turned out to be like Thailand. The major cities were modern and western, but the rural was still rural.

Regarding my mental state, I was not the same young American male that entered the air force in September 1960. My tours in Laos and the Joint Casualty Resolution Center changed me. I no longer believed in God, but now assigned to a country with religious zealots both Catholic and Islam, likewise, my respect for our government and leaders of the military barely existed.

Clark Air Base was the largest United States Air Base outside the continental United States. The base was so large, an air police horse patrol was required to assure security. Besides the air base, Clark had the finest, most sophisticated air to ground combat range in the world. (Aircrews from around the Pacific Command came to Clark to train and compete in war games to determine the best squadron in the Pacific Air Command).

At Poro Point, PI, the Department of Defense maintained an Air to Air Range for the same purpose as the Air-to-Ground Range. The Republic of the Philippines provided our country with an environment to train, but at what price.

Since I was a Master Sergeant, rank had some benefits. Due to the non-availability of adequate housing for senior non-commissioned officers, I, along with other airman of senior rank, was given a housing allowance to live off base. I chose the Oasis Hotel, in Angeles City, located outside of Clark's gates. Rooms had been renovated to the renters specifications. I had two hotel rooms made into one large apartment. After a short time, I had a live in girlfriend and a maid.

Cost of living in the Philippines provided Americans with benefits one could not receive in the United States. A number of dependent wives, living in base housing, had either live-in maids or day to day maids.

My duty assignment was to be at the 3rd Tactical Wing's Current Operations and Scheduling Division. Assigned tasks were to assure the publication of the weekly flying schedule and any/all publications pertaining to the wing's flight proficiency. Assist in the administrative process to ready the 3rd Air Wing to participate in the annual "Team Spirit" Exercise in South Korea. Tasked the Wing's Squadrons to provide aircrew members for ferry missions to the United States and Ping Tung, Taiwan. Beside the tasking of the squadrons, assured the altitude reservations, refueling support and any other requirement necessary for a safe aircraft delivery.

The chief of my division was a pilot I had served with a Kelly Air Force Base, Texas. His promotions had been advanced. Also Captain Rumble, the former Prisoner of War, was now Major Rumble. He was one of the scheduling officers.

Regarding the ferry missions to Ping Tung, Taiwan. The 3rd wing had one squadron of T-38 (F-5s) called the Aggressor Squadron. The squadron's aircraft were painted the color and marked with a red star to be recognized as Soviet Aircraft.

The squadron flew to different Pacific Air Bases to fight against U.S. Air Crews and participated in the war games at Clark against U.S. Squadrons. The reason for the flights to Ping Tung was the contractor's location that painted the aircraft to soviet specifications.

Ferries to the United States were to deliver aircraft to an Air Force Logistic Air Command Base for maintenance that were unable to be accomplished at Clark and/or to refit the aircraft with new systems.

Living off-base had its good and bad. My live-in was of mixed race. Her brother-in-law was a civilian technician at Poro Point. He was in charge of the launch and recovery of the drones used as mid-air targets for the fighter aircraft.

My live-in and I became very close and we complimented each other. It would be true to say that I loved her. For some the age disparity between us was a concern. However, right or wrong, I assumed she would be an outstanding step-mother for my son.

We were married. She was Catholic. My records and dog tags showed I was a Baptist. In truth, I was and am, an atheist. The wedding reception was held at my brother-in-law and sister-in-laws home at Poro-Point.

The best man was an air force Technical Sergeant Chuck Zull. Chuck was the NCOIC of the Scatback T-39 scheduling at the 3rd Tactical Fighter Wing.

The reception was exceptional. A large number of family members but, only Chuck and his girlfriend from Clark. Wow! The wedding cake and food was delicious.

Looking back at our time together, I have to fault myself for a lot of our problems. I was still in a state of anger, and I suppose, mentally strained, from which came a lot of profanity.

The only incident and/or event that I regret occurred when my section gave me a going away party, as I could not handle the number of people, the alcohol, smoke filled room, plus my wife kept demanding that we leave. For all I know she may have slept with one of the pilots before I met her. If so, it wouldn't bother me as women were there that I had slept with. My wife and I departed early.

Fortunately for me during one practice deployment exercise, my commanders knew and accepted the mental stress I was under. (I didn't realize and/or accept the fact until the 1990s). The incident was at the Military Airlift Passenger Terminal. Everyone was gathered in this big area after completing their administration part of the exercise. We were waiting for the boarding phase of the exercise.

After a period I became really agitated. The crowd gathered in the room. Too me, I did not know what was going to happen, if the exercise had been a real deployment to Osan Air Base, Republic of Korea. Too many acted as if the whole thing was a joke. It wasn't a joke. I couldn't take anymore and returned to my office.

The war between the United States, South Korea against North Korea and China ended in a truce. One side or the other could announce withdrawal from the truce at any given date or time. In fact, North Korea, during May or June 2009 declared the truce was over.

Military personnel knew from day one, that once hostilities broke out between the North and South, the North Koreans would over run Seoul, DMZ, and Osan Air Base. The 3rd Tactical Fighter Wing would deploy to Osan, once Osan had been retaken by the United Nations Forces. The 3rd Wing would begin air operations against North Korea. My experience in Laos taught me the grounds at Osan would be littered with the dead from gunfire, bombs, chemical weapons and you name it. The stink of the environment would make our personnel sick unless they brought gas masks. Was is not a exercise. People die, civilizations lost. Moreover, wars should never be fought unless your very civilization is at risk. Religious crusades do not justify war.

As I mentioned earlier, during my assignment at Clark, I established a rapport with an American citizen (Technical Sergeant), born in Jamaica. He had a Thai lady companion. He had been the Non-Commissioned Officer of the Scotback Operations (VIP oriented and high headquarters tasked flights), at Nakhon Phanom Royal Thai Air Base during the Mayaquez incident. And, as I wrote, he agreed U.S. State Departments abuse of their powers resulted in unnecessary American deaths during Mayaquez.

A decade or so past, I wrote the Chairman of the Joint Chiefs of Staff concerning Clark Air Base. My point was Clark was not worth the demonstrations, eventual anguish of Airman forced to marry an indigenous woman (no, I was not forced), the crime committed against Americans charged of Rape (of course there may have been some), and the thefts both on and off-base of American property. The government of the United States should have heeded history, as to why we gave the Philippines her independence.

Should anyone I knew or knew of me, at Clark Air Base read this book, I apologize for my anger and/or acts that may have been unbecoming.

Travis Air Force Base, California

Wouldn't you know it. My follow-up and last assignment in the United States Air Force turned out to be Travis Air Force Base, California. I had been to the base's Military Airlift Command's passenger terminal so many times since Travis was port of departure for the Pacific Air Forces Command, but never permanent party. This time, I would be bringing a wife and a young son.

The assignment was to the 60th Military Airlift Wing (MAW), one of several Air Wings assigned to 22nd Air Force. (The numbered air force, 22nd, was located at Travis. The 22nd Air Force was responsible for all military transportation missions from West of the Mississippi River to Tehran, Iran. The 22nd was also responsible for logistic mission to the Antarctica. The 21st Air Force was responsible for flights East of the Mississippi to Tehran.

A unique situation took place at Travis, In my opinion, regarding duty assignment. I was a Master Sergeant with the skill level of an Air Operations Superintendent. At Travis there were a couple more Air Operations Superintendents that were either Senior Master Sergeants or Chief Master Sergeants. I was surprised when I was made the 60th MAW Current Operations Superintendent.

I soon found out the reason I was selected for the position. None of the other superintendents wanted the position. Why? Allegedly, the Chief of Current Operations, an Air Force Lieutenant Colonel was a person no one wanted to work for, or with. I soon found out why. In my opinion, he was a poor supervisor, did not meet the standards of an Officer and Gentleman, I believe he was prejudiced against people of color.

The position at Current Operations entailed making sure the administrative tasks were completed timely and professionally. Assigned were a number of scheduling officers, plus several enlisted personnel. Our division tasked the flying squadrons with air support missions charged to our wing by higher quarters, plus the Antarctica Missions. The schedulers would write out the name of the squadron, build the flight plan, and make whatever administrative task that had to be accomplished. Then the schedulers would turn the paper trail over to the enlisted person. The enlisted Airman would type the information, via a pony circuit teletype system to the applicable squadron. I was doing pretty much the same job I did at the 3rd Tactical Fighter Wing at Clark Air Base, Republic of the Philippines.

With the years of experience behind me, I introduced the section and enlisted airman to the teletype tape system. Since most of the airlift missions were pretty much the same, we made sample tapes. When the airman received the flight documents, he would choose the correct tape and send out the tasking information to the applicable squadron. Any changes to the new mission versus the sample tape was amended by simply stopping of the formatted tape, type in the dew data, then turn the formatted back on. Task completed with much less time and effort.

The office environment was not the best in the world between the Lt. Colonel and myself. On a particular day, he offended a black sergeant assigned to current operations. The sergeant told me about the incident and I spoke to the Lt. Colonel. Not satisfied, I went to the 60th Wing's Director of Operations regarding the incident.

I suppose we both were punished in some way. I was reassigned to a more senior position as the Current Operations Superintendent at the 22nd Air Force Headquarters. The Lt. Colonel's retirement, allegedly, was expedited.

Digress a bit. Soon after I settled in at the 60th MAW position, I wrote Air Force Headquarters and requested retirement on 30 September, 1980. The air force came back and said I would have to stay on active duty until 01 October, 1980 for retirement pay purposes. I agreed. A short time later, I received a letter from HQ, AF asking me to become a First Sergeant. I had to refuse.

My wife, son, and I arrived at Travis from leave in Michigan and Kentucky. We picked up my son in Detroit and visited my younger sister in London, KY. The base assigned us to the family transient facilities until we could find housing. A short time later, really short, we received notification we would be moving into base housing, where the senior officers and senior non-commission officers resided.

A wonderful home. Our house was on a small hill facing the roadway. Our neighbors were terrific. However, soon after moving in, my sister-in-law's two children came from Poro Point, PI to live with us., This event was nice as the children were no problem whatsoever. However, the mother was a problem, as in my opinion, she had no morals whatsoever. Her husband was back in the Philippines and she was in California dating a senior non-commissioned officer. Not a good example.

My wife was raised by her sister, which probably explains my wife's morals and/or lack their of. In fact, my wife believes her sister is actually her mother.

We did not know any families on base or in the Fairfield area. After becoming acquainted with base personnel, I learned the controller that called me from being besieged site in Laos was the senior Non-Commissioned Officer in Charge of the Combat Control Section.

My wife soon found a Filipino who was married to a non-commissioned officer assigned to the Combat Control Team. A non-

Filipino turned into a nightmare for me. The lady was originally from the country of Turkey and was married to a non-commissioned officer. His religion was Mormon.

The lady from Turkey helped us in many ways since we were new to Travis. However, the bad outweighed the good. My wife and her started going out in the evenings. Soon I learned her Turkey friend was pregnant and it was not her husbands. The night that my wife came in from another night out, not with the Turkish woman, but with an officer nurse from the base hospital, I was sitting in a chair watching television when she approached me and confided in me that she liked women. The news was not a complete surprise.

I had no problem with her having a woman lover, an Air Force Nurse, since my penis didn't work all the time. Even when it did, it wasn't the penis of my younger years. I started to have Erectile Difficulties in Laos. At least I knew she was not going to get pregnant like the Turkish woman. My feelings for her never changed and she was an outstanding step-mother to my son. (In truth, she was an excellent housekeeper, cook, military wife, and lover, when I was able. She did not know herself. from listening to her childhood, that we Americans are not the only ones that grew up in an unhealthy household).

We were finally able to purchase our own automobile. (I paid for her to attend drivers school at Clark Air Base, Philippines. She is an outstanding driver). One day, I don't remember how I learned, but my wife had a vehicle accident with an air police vehicle near the base commissary. I worked that incident out.

Relationship with my son and her ended. One day she found a sandwich under his bed. She started beating my son. (She had terrible migraine headaches). I stepped in front of her. I told she could whip our son, but not beat him. She called the air police.

Soon afterward, she told me she was pregnant. I told her I did not want the child. She then took an extended vacation back to the Philippines where she, allegedly had the abortion. When she returned, a few months remained until I would be retired from the U.S. Air Force. My son had returned to Michigan to reside with my aunt and go to school.

Mother nature was with me again. One day while eating downtown, the party and I met an individual who had worked for Northrop in the Kingdom of Saudi Arabia. I was interested and submitted a resume. I received an offer for a non-accompanied employment to King Khalid Air Base, Khamis Mushayt, Asir Province, Kingdom of Saudi Arabia.

The company was Northrop Aircraft Services with a position as Air Operations Supervisor. My wife remained in Fairfield with a single Filipino woman and her children. Her nurse friend was still on active duty at Travis.

Over the next, almost ten years, we spent more time separated than together. She, allegedly, lived in a convent for a period, stayed with a woman in Wisconsin, share my home in Arizona with a male lover, and married to the Air Force Officer she was living with near McChord Air Force Base, Washington. She and her husband have a teenage daughter.

The command structure at 22nd was good enough to allow me to take the assignment with Northrop while I was on terminal leave.

There is no organization in the world better than the United States Air Force. I know the air force really took care of me. I was truly messed up both physically and mentally at retirement. They (air force) did not leave me behind.

Middle East
Saudi Arabian Experience

After accepting the employment offer by Northrop, and with all the negative news one hears and reads about the Middle East, I was optimistic about the employment assignment. It was my desire to learn the truth about the Middle East.

Palestine (Canaan) and Arabia were the birth place of Judaism, Christianity, and Islam. Religion had been, to use a common term, forced down my throat from the time I could talk to my departure from home during September 1960.

Even before the six non-consecutive years that I resided in Saudi Arabia, plus the visits to Egypt, Italy, and Greece. I knew the religious propaganda that I was taught, was just that - propaganda.

As a young boy, and then a teenager, I questioned in my mind the stories told in Bible School, at Sunday Church Service, and mandatory periods to hear money hungry fax ministers preach at revivals.

Throughout my life, I have been independent, and questioned just about everything, but to learn the truth I read historical and scientific studies. The school library subscribed to National Geographic, Popular Mechanics, and multiple services of world books and almanacs.

My career in the military did not afford assignment to the Middle East or Europe. I did have the opportunity to fly from Laos the Madrid,

Spain with an operational over-night stop in New Delhi, India. From Madrid, I flew to Majorca, a large island approximately 100 miles East of the Spanish coast. The island is a Spanish possession. I spent two weeks traveling the island and enjoying the beach.

I was assigned to the Republic of the Philippines, and the Kingdom of Thailand, which have a minority population of Muslims. The Philippines was the only country at the time to have trouble with the Muslims. The weapons providers, and instigators of trouble were Communist China, not an Arab state.

The countries identified at the time of my visit was not under Control of Muslim Religious Zealots, but Muslim influence of Arab culture could not be denied.

At the receipt of the position with Northrop, it was illogical Arabs, and their environment that could be as bad as the news pundits published in the U.S. Jewish controlled news media.

Northrop brought all new employees to Hawthorne, California. At Hawthorne, we emulated our years in the military for processing in at a new assignment. More detailed were the heads up classes to teach us Arab customs, and instill into us the do's and don'ts in-country.

Like the U.S. Air Force emphasized regarding our presence in-country, we were representing the United States of America. Northrop Aircraft Services Division had the same lectures.

Of note, the history of the Northrop Corporation was a true story of willing to work, thus succeeding. The corporation was one of the largest military contractors in the United States. Alleged, the President of the Northrop Corporation was under indictment, or some type of legal action by the U.S. Congressman. Allegedly, the President paid a bribe to an influential Saudi, to confirm the sale of Northrop's F-5 aircraft to the Royal Saudi Ministry of Defense and Aviation.

My first after retirement employment, was to be unaccompanied. In truth, we probably did not have a marriage. We cohabitated together, for infrequent periods. She did her thing, and I worked to provide the three of us with an excellent life.

Leave it to me to do one of the acts that we were told not to do. While waiting for our flight to Saudi Arabia, I spoke with a lot of people. Some of them happened to be Arab women from Saudi Arabia. They all were wearing western women's clothing. Some even had their hands and feet painted with colorful designs, which was the custom. I even acknowledged their presence onboard the aircraft. However, upon entering Saudi Arabian airspace, Saudi attire appeared, and their western clothing was covered. My first taste of Arab culture.

The customs and culture training at Northrop was interesting and somewhat factual, but allow me to present a true picture of the Kingdom of Saudi Arabia. The perception is from six non-consecutive years of dealing with individuals in all economic and social levels of the Saudi Arabian population.

First of all, and most important, is the King of Saudi Arabia has many titles. The most important is "The Custodian of the Holy Mosques."

The Mosques are located in Mecca, Medina, and Jerusalem. Since King Abdullah ascended to the Saudi Throne, the Jerusalem Mosque, known as the Dome of the Rock, has been eliminated from the title.

The King is the Supreme ruler, and religious leader of the country.

However, during my stay, all citizens do not consider themselves Saudi's.

The King is not their leader. Their leaders are the tribal chief or clan head. The same situation as our country found in Iraq. Government means nothing other than an avenue to deal with the international community.

Most of the international community does not understand that the Kingdom of Saudi Arabia is self-reliant in the production of wheat, poultry, meat, and dairy products. The population centers have malls, stateside supermarkets, and U.S. Fast Food Chains. Anything you want from the West. I mean anything. If you have the money, the item is yours.

Zionist in the United States, Europe, and some Latin American countries are the source of the untruths regarding the Arab race, and Islam. I do not like to use the word hate because I do not believe in hate, but for the religious zealots, hate is as common as apple pie.

Zionist (Christians and Jews) are the true enemy of the International community, not individuals of other religions, or the non-religious.

The Kingdom provides all foreign employees with an English copy of the Holy Koran. It is up to the employee to take time and learn the truth about Islam. Whether Zionist want to admit the fact or not, Islam is a plagiarized version of Judaism and Christianity.

The God of Abraham, Moses, and Jesus are all players in the Torah, the Bible, and Koran. Jews claim their Arab ethnic group is God's Chosen People. Christians believe an individual cannot enter heaven without first believing in Jesus Christ. Muslims believe there is but one God, and Allah is that God. Each religion had to have a printed advantage over the other Arab ethnic groups to assume superiority in the community.

The Kingdom is attempting to take the country to a monarchy type government like Great Britain. However, the King would still remain the Supreme Government and Religious Leader. There would be a House of Commons, and the House of Lords. A Prime Minister would be the day to day administrator of Saudi laws and policies.

One has to remember Saudi Arabia is a young country. The country is less than one hundred years as a united country, under the leadership of the House of Saud. Must we forget, our country is two hundred plus yeas in being, and yet, we are still trying to work out violations of the United States Constitution.

The violations that I speak of refer to the last eight years of the George W. Bush and Richard Cheney Presidential Administration. With the three traitors, in my opinion, our government became a monarchy government. The President was King. The Vice President was the Prime Minister. The U.S. Senate was the House of Lords, and the U.S. House of Representatives were the House of Commons.

In my opinion, George W. Bush was mentally unstable. Richard Cheney was a corporation hatchet person, that had no respect or loyalty to the United States. Bush dispatched troops to Iraq in a Religious Crusade against Islam and Saddam Hussein. Cheney's purpose in life was to make the Presidency a monarchy, and allow the bankers and corporations to succeed in their quest for unlimited power and money.

It is amazing that on this day, June 25, 2009, in history, Republicans and Democrats are in an uproar concerning the election in Iran. How hypocritical, as Bush was awarded the Presidency by the U.S. Supreme Court. Please!

Now to return to Northrop employment.

After clearing customs in Jeddah, Saudi Arabia, we were taken to a hotel maintained by Northrop, for transient personnel. One fixture in the bathroom caught my attention, was the hot water heater. In our country, normally hot water is heated in a large, metal cylinder type apparatus. In Saudi Arabia, hot water is heated by an open gas flame. Water runs from the pipe, while the gas heats the pipe and the water.

Television programs were provided b pre-programmed video tapes. The company had a company television section that provided the community with U.S. news, and video movies.

The Saudi driver also acted like a guard.

For your interest, in Saudi Arabia it is against the law to take a picture of any government building.

Following the over-night in Jeddah, we returned to the airport, what an experience, and boarded Saudi to Abha, Asir Province, Saudi Arabia. We were met by a Northrop representative, and driven to the Northrop compound. The compound was located on King Khaild Air Base. Both the U.S. and Saudi military lived on the compound. Americans on one side, and Saudis on the other. Saudi homes, later in my tour, had walls built to surround their homes. There was a mosque on the compound. The call to prayer was a vocal expression we became familiar with.

Personal identification cards and travel documents were the norm in the Kingdom. One did not travel without written consent in some form and/or document.

The base housing was exactly like U.S. Air Force Base Housing in the Southwest. Many of the families were retired military with Thai, Lao, and Philippino wives. I truly felt at home. The houses were ranch type, and fully furnished. Northrop had a community club, with a miniature golf course. There was an American Department of Defense school, library, and swimming pool. If you didn't know you were in Saudi Arabia, you could not tell by your environment.

The Northrop Community was probably the best living environment of my life. Nobody tried to take advantage of you. Every employee was there for the same purpose - train the Royal Saudi Air Force. Besides the amenities addressed previously, an employee's wife from Oklahoma ran the barber shop and beauty shop, plus she was the go to person on the base if you needed anything. She produced and directed a stage play, in which I participated.

Speaking of participation, Northrop had a community day each year. We set up booths, like at a county fair, had drawings for free gifts, and the international community of government contractors were invited to attend. The evening of the fair, a party was held in the multi-purpose building. There was music and dancing. Even the Saudi Base Commander, his wife, and other Saudi guests attended.

I arrived at King Khalid Air Base, a thirty six year old Air Force retiree, on terminal leave. I thought my future was fixed with the Department of Defense Contract Job with Northrop. However, my twenty years in the Air Force, at the non-Air Force installations, and air bases that did not meet the environment standards of the U.S., my body functions broke down within weeks of my arrival at King Khalid.

Mother nature turned against me. The bowel troubles that I had while stationed in the Republic of the Philippines, and at Travis Air Force Base, California returned. I had to immediately use the bathroom after each meal. I had terrible cramps, and the occasional blood in my stool, and commode water.

A lucky day for me occurred one day in the squadron, when the retired British Air Force Colonel Flight Surgeon, and now the squadron's flight surgeon, was in the squadron. While in the bathroom, this day saw darker blood in the water, and toilet paper. I took a piece of the toilet paper, and showed it to the flight surgeon. He confirmed that it was blood.

The reason I wrote about the blood, is that at Travis, the days when blood was in the commode water, I thought it was from eating a pasta meal with tomato sauce. The P.A. at the hospital never had a stool sample check. So, I was glad that the flight surgeon was in the squadron.

From the squadron, I went to Northrop's compound, and was hospitalized. Northrop's doctor ran tests, but could not come up with a diagnosis.

Northrop Corporation had a contract with a hospital in Athens, Greece to support in-country medical needs of Northrop employees. So, off I flew to Greece. The Greek doctors ran tests, and came up with a diagnosis, and treated me for it. I returned to King Khalid, and the bowel problems, with blood, returned as I did. This trip, the Northrop doctor arranged for me to go to Weisbaden Air Force Hospital, and Landstuhal Army Hospitals in Germany. Americans doctors found, as the Northrop doctor had suspected, that I suffered from Ulcerative Colitis.

Due to the steroids prescribed by the American doctors in Germany, I had to stop at the Weisbaden hospital en-route back to the United States.

I had completed my contract, and returned to my home of record, which was in Trenton, Florida (Trenton was the home of my daughter). The Air Force had stored my household items for the stay in Saudi Arabia, and they were transported back to Trenton. Also, coming to Trenton was my wife at the time. My plan failed.

Prior to leaving King Khalid, I said goodbye to all my friends, regardless of nationality, especially the lady that ran the community, and my Southeast Asian friends. I kissed one Thai lady (I had deep feelings), on the cheek.

At a later assignment at King Khalid, this time with McDonnell Douglas, I learned that I was supposed to have had sexual affairs with a number of wives, especially the Thai women, while I was with Northrop. That was not true. I did not commit adultery. Another factor, even if I had chosen to commit adultery, an attempt would have proven embarrassing, as my erectile dysfunctional problem had become worse. So, no to everyone. I did not have sexual intercourse at King Khalid.

My first employment, with Northrop at King Khalid was the best, and most rewarding of the six non-consecutive years spent at the air base training Saudi Warrant Officers.

I arrived at King Khalid in September 1980, at a time when the United States was truly in bed with the Royal Saudi Government. Our government did not care who they went to bed with. We were supplying the Iraqi government with military logistics. Allegedly, the reason we assisted Iraq was to kill Iranians.

Iraq was such a good bed partner during the 1980s that on January 8, 007, Newsweek reported the following "So strong was Washington's "tilt" toward Saddam that in 1987, when one of his jet fighters launched a missile strike on a U.S. frigate in the Persian Gulf killing 37 sailors, the United States accepted his excuses, and responded by stepping up pressure on his enemies in Iran."

Northrop's employment tenure saw me in the position as the 15th Fighter Squadron (F-5 aircraft) Air Operations Supervisor. With two other employees with me, our task was to train Royal Saudi Air Force Warrant Officers in the Air Operations Vocation and Gun Camera Maintenance & Film Processing. Besides the three Americans, also assigned to the squadron was a British Flight Surgeon. Most of the Saudi pilots, I worked with in the early 1980s, I also worked with again on succeeding assignments with McDonnell Douglas Services F-15 aircraft.

My training program was a success. I tailored the Northrop Training Curriculum from the training package, and methods that I used at Kelly Air Force Base to training U.S. Air Force Cross-Trainees. We were successful with our efforts. I was selected as Northrop's Trainer of the Quarter, plus my training booklet was adopted for use by the Royal Saudi Air Force.

The first employment with McDonnell Douglas Services, at King Khalid Air Base, was accompanied. However, prior to our selection for the assignment, my wife and I had to be interviewed by the McDonnell Douglas employment team in St. Louis, MO. After we were accepted, I attended McDonnell Douglas Training Supervisor Course, in St. Louis. Only the SHADOW knew where my wife was while I was in school.

When my wife, son, and I arrived at King Khalid Air Base, our quarters, and community buildings were located across the road from Northrop's Compound.

The site of McDonnell Douglas' Compound was once a large empty land space, scattered with debris, including discarded fifty gallon drums. What was in the drums, who Knows? A Dutch company built the new compound, that was like Northrop's. It was home for both Americans and Saudis.

Once again, the Western style condo homes were fully furnished, with everything one would need to maintain a household.

My wife stayed for a short time with my son and I, then she returned to the United States to get her U.S. Citizenship (My employment on a U.S. Government Contract eased the rules for her to become a citizen). While she was with me, she was an ideal politician's wife. We had parties attended by the U.S. Air Force, and other employees of both companies. With my ED, it was hard for me to have sexual intercourse, so her sexual interludes, with one or more of the dependent wives, did not phase me (If she had sex with other men, I remain in the dark). I was then, and now, a shell of a man, when you cannot function as a man. My mind remained clear, but as of June 25, 2009, I am loosing my short term memory.

Prior to the completion of the employment assignment, my son had been involved in unsuitable acts, at the American school, plus he became angry and wanted to return to Detroit. He returned to Detroit while the three of us were in Paris. My wife and I returned to the Kingdom, but she remained only for a short time.

My rapport with Saudi officers, and enlisted personnel was outstanding. We could sit and talk about every subject: religion, politics, U.S. women, the United States, Saudi Arabia, etc. without anyone losing their temper. The conservations were truly candid. Most of the officers had been to the United States to attend flight school, the war college, etc.

Opinions of the United States varied. Some of their complaints were amusing. For example, they complained about alcohol consumption, drug use, and the loose women available for sexual intercourse. Saudi Arabia was no different. If you had the money, you could get anything you wanted. In fact, one of the most vocal pilots (expert pilot) used marijuana frequently.

The Hubble Bubbly pipes they smoked gave them a high from the product they smoked. Also, there was a piece of some type plant that they chewed that was a narcotic (You may remember a revolt the United States had to deal with in Somalia, when the U.S. attempted to stop the use of a plant. Same plant).

At completion of the first McDonnell Douglas contract, accompanied with my wife, we returned to Mesa, Arizona. We purchased a home, and my son moved in with my wife and I.

I received another job offer from McDonnell Douglas, but this one was unaccompanied. After a short period at King Khalid, I received notification that my son had run away from home, and returned to Detroit. Allegedly the reason my son ran away was because he had spilled Kool-Aid on our white stairway carpet. Supposedly, my wife became angry and beat my son with a candlestick holder.

I was given leave by the company, and I returned to the United States. Events with her had gotten out of hand, I told her that I wanted a divorce. Got the shaft again. I do not have any luck with women.

In hindsight, I should have stayed with her even though I could never know, who or what person she was having an affair with (Her sister's husband remained with his wife, even though her acts were the same with men as my wife's). She treated me like a husband, gave me sex, when I could get an erection, or allowed me to pleasure her in other ways. She was truly genius, in handling money and monetary affairs. I still love her, if love is the word. No! I couldn't - HIV is too dangerous.

My son continued his rebellion in Detroit. He came to live with me a couple of years past, but I had to make him move. His life-style, and fear of labor, do not meet my standards. But, that's life.

My last employment assignment at King Khalid, I requested it myself, by writing the F-15 Squadron Commander (This was the end of the 1980s). During one of my conversations with McDonnell Douglas Supervisor (After I had been on base for a short time), the Supervisor told me that the company did not want me to return to King Khalid. I was hired because of the F-15 Commander. The last I heard of the Commander, a number of years past, was that he was now a General, and Commander of Prince Sultan Air Base.

Looking back, I should have known, the war with Iraq was coming. The American environment at King Khalid was not the same as my other assignments. The U.S. Air Force advisors no longer had the zeal and spirit other former advisors did. The contract for domestic support, housekeepers, cooks, laundry persons, etc. was no longer held by an American company. The contract was with an Arab company, and allegedly, one member of the Royal family. Nothing was the same.

As the Squadron's Administrative Assistant - Operations, I worked with the non-indigenous employees, as well as the indigenous each day.

The rapport that I established caused me to be the source for the non-indigenous to complain. Allegedly, the new domestic company was mixing potable, and non-potable water together for their employees to drink. They were not providing proper housing, not paying them, and worst of all, beating the employees. Regarding beating, I knew of a Sri Lankan that was beaten and deported. His crime was probably speaking out against the conditions. I addressed the complaints with the RSAF, U.S. Air Force Administrators, and the McDonnell Douglas leadership of King Khalid. No one did anything about the abuse. I resigned, and returned to the United States. I wrote a member of Congress of the situation.

Saudi Arabia is a friend of the United States of America, and without a doubt, would provide the oil that the United States requires, because of the word of the founder of the Kingdom of Saudi Arabia. The Saudi's are people of their word. Our politicians are Zionist, this includes the current Vice President of the United States - Joe Biden. A return to the principles of the United States Constitution, all members of the U.S. Congress would be removed from office, and the news media pundits would be in prison. You do not yell FIRE in a crowded room.

Interim Employment Between Saudi Arabia Assignments

As I identified previously, after my first employment assignment in the Kingdom of Saudi Arabia, I rented an apartment in Gainesville, Florida (Trenton, the home of my daughter, was a short distance from Gainesville). Our family household items had been is storage during the time that I was out of the United States. Allegedly, my wife was in Fairfield, California, and my son was in Detroit, with my Aunt Nora.

I truly was in both, mental and physical distress, when I arrived in Gainesville. I visited the Gainesville VA Medical Center to continue medication for Ulcerated Colitis. I hadn't sought medications or counseling for my mental health.

I do not know the reason, unless is was my mental health, that I could not obtain employment in Gainesville. Believe me, I sent resume after resume, and interviewed for several employment positions, but was apparently unemployable.

My wife came to Gainesville for a visit, but became impossible, when my ex-wife called the house, and identified herself as my wife. My ex-wife was married with a new child. No, the ex-wife and I did not, repeat did not, have sexual relations, as my daughter and wife assumed.

My wife returned to wherever with new money. $5,000.00 that I received from Northrop. Her departure came after she created a scene at the apartment.

In desperation, no job, and no money to sustain my apartment. I called my Father in London, Kentucky to come to Gainesville and pick me up (The reason for no military retirement money was while in Saudi Arabia, my wife received all of my military pay, except for allotments taken from said pay. I gave all our household items to a local religious organization. I took with me only my personal clothing and papers).

Since my Father and I didn't have the greatest rapport, life at his home was almost unbearable (You would have to know my Father). However, I was able to obtain employment at two separate locations, between return assignments back to Saudi Arabia.

One was with London's Storm Security Company. The owner was Mr. Storm. He had been my Physical Education Teacher at Lily High School. Outside of school, he coached Little League Baseball in London. I was on a team for awhile and I wasn't any good, but Mr. Storm allowed me to play occasionally.

Mr. Storm had a contract with Blount Construction, based in Alabama, with duty at one of the less congested tourist islands in the Bahamas. The Blount Company was building a new hotel that would rival the hotels on Paradise Island.

The construction company was having thefts at their site, and the possibility of physical abuse from the criminal element, Blount asked for a person to come down to the island to investigate.

With approximately 5 years experience in Law Enforcement and Security, plus a military degree in Law Enforcement and Security, I was hired to satisfy Blount's request.

Wow! Never been in the Bahamas, I was truly amazed at the island, the people, and Blount's Company. I stayed until we discovered who the culprits were, but most of all, I learned how amazing the people of the Bahamas were.

The last employment position in Kentucky, for which I was not suited, was as Kentucky's Pony Express Courier Corporations Supervisor. The position was in Lexington, KY, where I rented a room at one of the older, but clean motels, near the job site. The administrative function was not a problem, however, the non-military environment made me feel like a duck out of water. I resigned, without prejudice, within 90 days of starting the job.

From the Pony Express position, I returned to the Kingdom of Saudi Arabia with my wife and son. At the end of the employment, we returned to Mesa, Arizona, and rented an apartment. My wife departed again for another location, and my son went back to Detroit.

Luck was back, I was hired as a civilian employee of the U.S. Department of the Army, at the Phoenix Military Entrance Processing Station. The position was as a travel clerk.

As a travel clerk, I was responsible for the issuance of travel tickets and/or a military voucher to pay for their tickets, meal tickets, and hotel reservations for the new recruits. A video was made of me briefing new recruits, which was shown on a Phoenix Television Station. I was at this position for approximately 2 years, and then I returned to Saudi Arabia for another employment tenure.

Back to Arizona, from the unaccompanied assignment in Saudi Arabia. However, we now had a home in Mesa, Arizona, but due to a divorce, I moved into the same apartment complex that my family and I had resided previously.

Luck was with me again. I was hired as a Test Administrater at the Phoenix MEPS. I'm sorry to report, I was out of place dealing with young Americans taking the Military's Aptitude Test. We traveled around the state, even to the Mexican border, where some students from Mexico were tested. Mentally, I could not take the position.

Months went by without any response to resume's submitted, and job interviews. One day I learned from the newspaper's jobs section that a company was hiring for a summer job at a resort in Wyoming. I applied and was hired as a Housekeeping Supervisor. I completed my contract and moved to Detroit, to be with my Aunt.

Again, resume's submitted, and job interviews with a final good lead. I applied, was interviewed, and was hired as an officer clerk for the VA's Canteen Service. With my foot in the door at the Canteen Service, I applied for a position with the Department of Veterans, at Allen Park, Michigan. I was accepted.

The position at the VA was really interesting. I worked my way up to Mail Room Supervisor. Submitted a number of suggestions to save the VA money, improve efficiency, etc. My reward was a monetary award that allowed me a two week vacation in Sydney, Australia.

There is an old saying "You can take the person out of the mountain, but you can't take the mountain out of the person." I suppose this was my case. I volunteered to transfer to the Louisville VA Medical Center, and the transfer was approved.

Department Of Veteran Affairs

Some may say that to speak against the Department of Veteran Affairs (DOVA) is wrong. Back in the heyday of World War II, I would agree. But since, the U.S. Congress has set aside the United States Constitution to allow individuals like President Bush to take our nation into a Religious Crusade in Iraq, Afghanistan, Palestine, and Iran. I am comfortable with what I am, words.

What I learned from thirty five years of employment, mostly under the umbrella of the federal government, is that the U.S. military is the reason we remain, in some degree, the government that our founders envisioned.

The United States Navy is probably the most important military service, even though I served 20 years, and 1 day in the U.S. Air Force, of the United States Government. The Navy is the extended arm of the U.S. Government , in that this Air, Sea, and Land Force is capable of projecting our military might around the world. This power assures the United States of her physical security, keeps open the avenues for international commerce, and in time of disasters, delivers humanitarian services to the victims.

Not to reap the wrath of the possible reader of this chapter, I will address the other services.

The United States Air Force is the aerial transportation, and air defense branch of our governments military. Yes, in times of military conflicts, the Air Force shares the largest burden for aerial combat, air-to-ground sorties in some geographical areas, aerial transportation, and delivery of nuclear weapons.

The United States Army is the Army. As a standing Army, they defend on the ground, the United States from a physical invasion, and maintain anti-aircraft/missile sites to protect population centers, and the White House from the assorted modes of aerial attacks. However, today, as previously stated, Congress has set aside the United States Constitution.

The Marine Corps is a part of the U.S. Navy, so they are the primary ground force on-board carrier group, or designated expeditionary group assigned to a Commands area of responsibilities.

The United States Coast Guard is the least talked about, but is an equally important service in the preservation of the United States. The Coast Guard not only serves to protect the international boundaries of the United States, U.S. Ports, Waterways, etc., but they serve in combat environments with the same professionalism as Department of Defense services.

Prior to 1966, the Coast Guard was under the administration of the United States Treasury Department. At the cited year, the Coast Guard became part of the newly formed Department of Transportation.

It is my opinion, that President Obama should look at returning the defense structure of the United States back to the dictates of our founders. The industrial military complex has turned the United States into an aggressor nation.

President George W. Bush, 43, manipulated the truth to invade the only country that continued to pose a historical threat to the Socialist country of Israel - Iraq (The new Iraq will continue the historical contempt for the Arab Hebrews. This is why General Casey, Chairman of the Joint Chiefs of Staff, says that the United States will be in Iraq for ten more years). Bush's acts of aggression were not new, we witnessed the same misuse of government power during former President William Jefferson Clinton's Administration.

For those of us that keep abreast of current events, everyone knew that when the honorable Madeline Albright was appointed U.S. Secretary of State, the U.S. military would become more active. She was known as an advocate to use U.S. Armed Forces to impose United States' policies without regard to the United Nations, or the Congress of the United States.

Whether anyone agrees or not, the war in the Balkans was a religious war with a nationalist side bar. Yes, there were the unjustifiable killings of individuals because of their religion, and/or from which part of Yugoslavia they called home (Yugoslavia, like Iraq, was a nation composed of populations of different religions and cultures. Yugoslavia had President Tito, and Iraq had President Saddam Hussein. The two countries were held together by brute force).

Deep in my mind, I knew there had to be more to the Balkan War than nationalism and religion. I communicated with a Lord Stirling, a OEN columnist, and asked about my concern. Lord Stirling responded that the true cause was fossil fuels.

Kosovo has attained it's independence, and the oil companies have a new source of oil, gas, and coal. So what's new?

The Balkans War should have been resolved by the European Union, not the United States or NATO. There was no outside aggressor, except for the oil companies, and Jews in the government of the United States.

Furthermore, in my opinion, Secretary Albright was not concerned about the war between the warring parties in Yugoslavia, but the destruction of television and radio stations, automobile factories, and other industries owned by Jews.

What does the war in Iraq, and previous war in the Balkans have to do with the Department of Veteran Affairs? Answer: more wounded, injured American military personnel, requiring short and long term health maintenance from the Department of Veteran Affairs (DOVA).

Wait, on December 2, 1996, an article in the Air Force Times newspaper reported that military health benefits, as contracted, per the words of military recruiters, literature, etc., for those entering the military in 1960, were not affordable. Yet on October 9, 1996, Congress enacted Public Law 104-262. This law virtually eliminated eligibility prerequisites for health care, and to eliminate the hospitalization clause for the non-service connected military veteran. Public Law dated September 1980 was void.

The welfare class of former two year former military members, or those individuals that did not care, or both to become employed to earn a source of income for retirement , pushed aside the Service Connected military veteran.

What is a military veteran? After September 1980, an individual entering the Armed Forces of the United States had to serve for two consecutive years in the Armed Forces to receive VA Health Care. The veteran had to receive an Honorable, or Under Honorable Conditions Discharge. Likewise, should a member of the Reserves or National Guard be activated, on written orders from the President of the United States for a national emergency, the two years was not applicable. For example: The Persian Gulf War from November 1990 - April 1991.

The Veteran Administration's original premise, as envisioned by two former Presidents, Abraham Lincoln and Theodore Roosevelt, was to care for the military person that had shed his blood on the battlefield, and borne the battle in defense of our great nation. Not only would the veteran be cared for, but his dependents would benefit from his/her courage and actions.

The two classifications of the Veteran Administration that I learned while working there are: Service Connected (SC), and Non-Service Connected (NSC).

1. SERVICE CONNECTED: To my knowledge, Service Connected meant that the member had to be wounded, injured, or a known existing ailment that was aggravated by conditions/events incurred while in the military.
2. NON-SERVICE CONNECTED: To my knowledge, Non-Service Connected meant an individual that had served in the military, and did not meet the prerequisites as Service Connected, was then categorized as Non-Service Connected.

Prior to 1996, the NSC person was eligible for hospitalization care only. Being assigned to a VA Clinic, and a VA Medical Provider did not qualify an individual for chronic medications, prosthetics, and dental care.

The NSC person pay for service care was divided into sectional tiers: One tier had to pay the established government charge for medications and health care. The second tiered person received all medications and care gratis. Third tier, allegedly, consists of homeless, housebound, pensioners, and veterans who are considered below the poverty level - everything is gratis.

What is illogical to me is when I worked at the VA Medical Center, and even today, if the policy has not been changed, it was/is: The military retiree (20 years plus), unless a Service Connected Veteran, is a NSC person subject to billing by the Department of Veteran Affairs for services rendered.

What we have, as partially stated earlier, we have an individual that was in the U.S. Military, for lets say, two years, he was given a discharge examination, and found to be in good health. After his discharge, he chose to live off of another person, not work, gamble, etc. Then he becomes ill, or attains the age of retirement. He has no money, health care, or a home. So he goes to the Veteran Administration, and receives a Non-Service Connected Pension. His medical, mental, and dental care is gratis. If needed, he will be assisted in obtaining a place of residence.

The career military person, for whatever the reason, did not pursue a physical or mental ailment, because he/she obtained employment after retirement, and the employer had health insurance that would cover the veteran, and his family for all medical related ailments. For some reason, like the current environment, the career person is laid off from work, and loses his medical. Oops, he becomes ill. He is taken, or drives to the nearest VA Medical Center for care. He's forced to provide the admissions person with his financial history. If his retirement pay is over a said amount, the career person will have to pay the Veterans Administration for his care, even though a career person was promised lifetime medical care without reservations.

Recalling back to September 1960, when I joined the Air Force, I do not recall the recruiter, or Air Force literature stating that you could remain on active duty for a non-specific time, earn medical benefits, and a VA Pension. What was clearly emphasized was that the member had to serve as a career military person - 20 years or more.

When I worked at the VA Medical Center, approximately two thirds of the individuals requesting care from the Department of Veteran Affairs were not Service Connected.

What the non-service numbers may indicate were part of the Clinton Administration's plan for a National Health System. The new VA policy allowed additional millions, mostly males, to have access to a government paid health program. Regrettably, unless the NSC person was permanently and totally disabled, his spouse could not even get an aspirin.

In my opinion, our government should establish a health care system for all Americans, if the Department of Veterans affairs is still viable based on the cost of only serving true military veterans (SC) and their dependents, then the vision of the two late presidents should remain intact. If not, the federal government should turn the DOVA (name change) into part of a government health program. No, the later would not work as true disabled veterans need care the NSC veterans were not subject to.

For the SC Veteran, the Veterans Disabled Card should entitle the veteran, in cases where authorized, his/her dependents could go to a doctor of their choice. However, any major medical ailment or surgery could be accomplished at the nearest VA Medical Center (In years past, the VA had a program that allowed certain veterans a FEE BASED Card. The Card allowed the selected veterans to do just as I proposed).

A personal dig. Should the Congress of the United States return to the U.S. Constitution, our nation would not be involved in military conflicts, except as the physical United States was attacked, and/or an exerted effort by a number of countries attempting to impede United States Commerce and international commerce.

Extremely personal for myself, and a couple of thousand more, is the denial by the Department of Veteran Affairs to honor disabilities incurred in the illegal war, in the Kingdom of Laos. For myself, an encounter with some type of herbicide is creating more medical problems for me each day.

Oh! Can someone tell me, what is behind the door, at both the Louisville and Lexington VA Medical Center, that reads "Minority Veteran"? What the hell is a minority veteran?

Israel, Judaism, & Zionism

I recall from summer Bible school, the Arab Hebrews (now known as Jews, based on their faith - Judaism), were always revolting against the legitimate rulers and community leaders of the land known as Palestine.

Nothing has changed in over 5,769 years (the years should be correct, within a decade or so). International Jewry is instigating domestic and political turmoil in Georgia, the Ukraine, Venezuela, Iran, and Cuba, to name a few. However, the Jewry has learned a better use for it's money. They bought the Congress of the United States of America. It is the American military man and woman dying or becoming maimed, for a greater Israel.

June 27, 2009, the Op News Network reported that Israel increased it's military presence at the border with Lebanon. Merkava tanks armored vehicles, and other weaponry, plus an increase in over-fly violations of Lebanon by the Israeli Defense Forces (IDF) are cursors of probable military action by Israel against Lebanon.

Several weeks passed, the IDF did a practice run to work out probable problem areas in their forthcoming bombing raid against the sovereign nation of Iran.

In the approximate time period, the Russian born Foreign Minister of Israel declared Israel would attack Iran within three months. The day is drawing nigh.

Zionist (Christians and Jews) in Congress, Old Testament Christians and the White House, as of January 5, 2007, are responsible for the deaths of 3,006 American military personnel, and 25,000 wounded in Iraq. Of the 25,000 wounded, are 10,000 who sustained such injuries, as they will never be able to obtain the quality of life that is the dream of every American.

Without a doubt in my mind, the aerial attack on the United States on September 11, 2001 was the under the radar expertise of Israeli Government agencies, Americans, such as Vice President Richard Cheney, and specific Jews in New York that would benefit from such an act.

Without assistance from the Executive Branch, the act could not have been carried forward. The United States has the best air defense and internal security than any other nation, overall in the world. By what authority did the Vice President of the United States be in charge of a National air defense exercise? He didn't. He doesn't.

No. President Bush could not award him such authority. According to the U.S. Constitution, the Vice President of the United States is without presence until the death of the President, and/or when the President signs over power to the Vice President to be acting President. Usually for an illness or surgery.

If we still had military leaders in the Pentagon, Cheney would not have been in charge of any exercise. As a retired military person, I knew Chairman Meyers was without integrity or balls.

I'm sorry that I drifted away from my discussion of those individuals whose religion is Judaism.

My personal belief, based on a lot of research, is that Abraham, the Hebrew, allegedly, the first Jew, was born in Ur (present day Iraq). Literature reveals that he was a wealthy man, with a large clan of family members. With his money, he owned herds of animals that needed food and water. Of course, we learned that he had one slave with whom he had sexual intercourse. It is only logical that he owned more than one slave.

What so many do not point out is that Ur was a major educational, and commerce center at this particular date in history. It would only be logical that Abraham would have known of the one Egyptian Pharaoh that attempted to establish one religion. The Sun God.

Again, it is logical that an educated man and/or woman could go and do whatever they pleased in the rural areas of the desert, and ungoverned land areas. Remember, literacy was a trait of the rich or royalty. Regrettably, the same is true today in too many parts of the Middle East.

We learned the Ur area suffered a bad drought, which would have forced wealthy families to move their herds, families, and slaves to a location where the animals could graze, and have water to drink. Individuals like Abraham were nomadic people, who had no concept of law and order, or with the humanity to spare human life.

Allegedly, from what I read, and was told by so many money hungry clergy, Abraham attempted on three occasions, to enter Palestine (Canaan). We know Babylon, or whatever the name of the power at that date in history, was a walled city with laws that induced moral responsibility. The city/nation had the Tigris, and Euphrates Rivers with other sources of water to sustain the Cradle of Civilization. Abraham and his clan were unable to bribe, or pull the religious scam on the leaders of Babylon.

The people of Palestine were made up of different Arab tribes, or clans, just as in the city of Ur (Abraham did not rule Ur. He was only a parasite on the community). The indigenous race was Arab, as was Abraham.

Did the people of Palestine lack the knowledge Abraham possessed?

Were they not familiar with the ideal of township or a large community, under the leadership of a single person?

Since the indigenous of Palestine were Pagans, there was not an organized religion. Enter Abraham the Hebrew telling the people of Palestine, that he had spoken with a God, and that God told him to come to Palestine.

The Pagans were astounded that an Arab man would declare that he had spoken to a God. To further convince the Pagans, Abraham allegedly, offered to kill his son as an offering to the God of Abraham.

The Pagans accepted Abraham, and allowed him and his clan to remain in Palestine. Abraham, knowingly or not, established a religion where you have to pay dues to practice worshiping a non-existent religious entity.

Of note, it was the custom of the Nomadic tribes to marry from within their clan or tribe (I saw the same practice in Saudi Arabia in the 1980s. Oh, don't forget, that in some parts of the United States, cousins marry cousins). So being of the Arab race, Arab Hebrews (Jews) married within their tribes/clan until I believe, one of the De Rothschild's married outside his Jewish community.

So if the Jewish community attempted to remain Jewish, then how can anyone believe that Jews were the majority in Jerusalem, Judah, and Samaria? De Rothschild's marriage was centuries later in time.

Even today, Israel's Zionist leadership are concerned of the growth of the Arab populations in the West Bank, Gaza, and the Arab Israeli's. They fear with the higher birth rates among the Palestinians/Arabs, the Arab population will overtake Israel.

History reveals, at one time there were two cities Judah (Judea) and Samaria. Jews, because of their belief that they were God's chosen people claimed to be their own cities. Please, Judah and Samaria were International cities located on or near the trade routes. The population was mixed with not only Arabs, Hebrew Arabs, but Romans. King Herod was a converted Jew. He was in power at the behest of the Roman Empire.

With the rise of Christianity and Islam, the Jewish community became a true minority. Since Jews always declared that they were God's chosen people, they would not admit to being citizens of the country they didn't administer, or believed they administered. They were Jews, not Arabs (Reminds one of pre-World War I Germany, the United States, and Europe today).

Jews became alarmed. Those that believed, and claimed their superiority, fled Palestine for other parts of the world. The Arabs whose religion was Judaism, chose to remain in Palestine, where they were/are free to practice their religion.

The Arabs, in terms of history, were lucky. The United States did not exist at the time, so the did not have to worry about economic sanctions, or military actions being taken against them because they would not allow Jews to migrate to other countries.

The former Soviet Union received bountiful rewards from the United States Government, and the Israeli Government to allow Jews to depart the Soviet Union. Their (Jews) destinations were the United States, Germany, and Israel. These three countries provided them money, health benefits, first crack at employment, and to live in a free environment while remaining a Jew. Never a citizen with loyalty to their host countries.

Our government cannot provide health care for Americans, but can spend billions defending the racist, illegal country of Israel, and support Jews in the occupied land of the Palestinians.

With continuing battle of individuals, whose religion is Judaism, still clinging to the ideal that they may reside in a host country, and reap the same benefits as the indigenous. For example: Saturday, January 6,

2007, the Lexington Herald-Leader printed an article "Jews being driven out of Ghetto in Rome". Stop the presses. Are the Zionist going to force the President of the United States to send U.S. Forces to Italy to make sure Jews can maintain their air of superiority?

Jews that fled Palestine from the 6th century until the mid 1800s, began to move away from traditional religious orthodoxy. The leaders wanted to take the Jews from being Jews, into being a citizen of the country where they resided. The concept was for Jews to assimilate into the European communities as Europeans. It didn't happen, and even today, Jews do not assimilate.

Allegedly, an incident occurred in France in the late 1800s, that influenced one individual to re-kindle the air of Jewish superiority through an idea called Zionism.

Zionism's intent was to unite the Jewish people of the Dispaora (exile), and settle them in Palestine. Comparable to the Moses fable, telling his family and followers, to go into Canaan (Palestine) and kill everyone, except virgins. The land of Canaan was a gift from God.

Moses and his followers failed to forcefully take-over Palestine, but with the massive United States assistance the Israeli military took over Palestine in 1967. With the take over of Palestinian territory and East Jerusalem, a person of Judaism meant: (1) The autonomy and safety of the state of Israel. (2) The right of any Jew to settle in Israel (LAW OF RETURN). The two statements provide a guarantee of Jewish Nationality to any Jew in need of it.

The Zionist movement resulted in an exodus of intellectuals from their countries of citizenship, and drainage of monetary resources from countries around the world to support the questionable immigration to a land belonging to the Palestinian people. For example:

(1). Baron Edmond J De Rothschild financially supported the Jews in Palestine from the Zionism's inception until his death in 1934.

(2). Starting in 1929, two separate Jewish groups in the United States supported different fractions of the Zionist movement. One supported European Jews. The other supported the Jews in Palestine (I wonder if the departure of Jews in the United States to Palestine during the 1920s - 1930s, didn't cause the Great Depression or at the very least, enhanced the depression).

On January 3, 2007, the Lexington Herald-Leader Newspaper printed a column regarding the death of a former Jerusalem mayor, Theodor Kollek. The following are two different paragraphs regarding Mr. Kollek: "Name of the chief theorist of modern Zionism, Theodor Herzi. Mr. Kollek was born in Nagyvaszony, near Budapest, in 1911 and raised in Vienna. He immigrated to Palestine, then under British authority in 1934 he helped found Kibbutz Ein Gev on the shores of the Sea of Galilee.'

"During World War II, he worked to help European Jews escape Nazi persecution, securing the transfer of thousands from concentration camps to Great Britain. After the war, he organized weapons shipments to the nascent Jewish state's Armed Forces before the United Nations partition of Palestine in 1947."

In 1947, the Jews of Palestine demand for statehood was turned over to the United Nations (The British, during the United Nations Palestine Mandate, were unable to honor commitments to both Arabs and Jews for an independent state from the lands of Palestine). One should note that in April 1947, the Palestinians outnumbered the Jews, 1,300,000 to 600,000.

The Jews had a well equipped and trained army, made so by individuals like Mr. Kollek, wealthy Jews around the world, and even worse, countries like the United States and Great Britain allowed their Jewish citizens to fight against the indigenous Arabs (The same countries still allow their Jewish citizens to be a member of the Israeli Defense Forces (IDF), and after their military commitment is completed, they remain IDF Reserves).

Jews had established a semi-autonomous government with David Ben Gurion, as their leader. The Arab community had not recovered from an Arab revolt in 1936. Most of their leaders were in exile or prison. Whereas, there was no leadership to bring together. Most of the Arabs I met, would wander off into the desert, or find some excuse not to commit aggressive acts. Blue flu, etc.

Jews had the best military in the Middle East, and were manned by trained foreign military personnel from countries such as the United States, Europe, and Central/ South America. The Arabs did not have a chance.

I laugh out loud each time I hear the President, and the news media pundits call Arabs terrorists. The world's greatest terrorist were former Israeli Prime Ministers. These individuals were part of Jewish terrorist groups attacking the British, and killing Palestinians. For example, the Jewish terrorist blew up the King David Hotel that was a host for British Forces assigned in Palestine.

A Jewish British subject and military person, assisted the terrorist in blowing up the King David Hotel. He hid in another section of the hotel during the explosion. He also provided the terrorists with British troop movements, resulting in the wounding, and deaths of his fellow countryman for a fabricated religion.

Jewish terrorists soon became Prime Ministers (Two were Americans), leaders of the Israeli Defense Forces, and members of the Israeli Government. In 1967, when the Israelis attacked their neighbors, they also attacked the United States Ship Liberty, on station in International waters. Americans were killed and wounded. The Liberty had to be salvaged.

In the United States, Zionist care more for Israel and their religion, than they do the United States of America. It is/was the physical United States, and her citizens that made our country prosper. No God was visible or heard to control the events responsible for the U.S. becoming the leading military force in the international community.

I ask the religious community to identify which God they speak of, that did so much for the United States? For example, the God of Abraham is the God for those of Judaism, Christianity, and Islam.

Now to briefly comment on the TREASON by American Presidents. The United Nations sent an Ambassador to resolve the land dispute between the Arabs and Jews. Jewish terrorist ambushed and murdered the Ambassador. The United Nations withdrew.

Almost as bad, was the recognition of Israeli statehood by former President Harry S. Truman, within hours of the announcement. Supreme Soviet leader Joseph Stalin followed soon after Truman. The United Nations finally accepted Israel as a sovereign country in 1949.

With Israel, Judaism, and Zionism, I am confused, which is probably normal for me. The facts are, Judaism is a religion and not a race. You can become a Jew through birth, marriage, converting to Judaism, and I'm sure many more reasons. You have to give Zionists, Pat Robertson, Jerry Falwell, and James Dobson credit for turning the Red States, and the President of the United States into believers of a fabricated religion. Thus, a fabricated God.

Wait, religion with Jews is more than a religion. Take for example: The Jews in the United States Senate and U.S. House of Representatives, use their chairmanship to committees, to funnel money to Jewish groups subverting foreign governments. The most recent case identified, was in a USA Today news article on June 27, 2009. Two of the statements from the news brief were: (1). "U.S. efforts to support Iranian opposition groups have been criticized in recent years, as veiled attempt to promote "regime change," said Trita Parsi, President of the National Iranian American Council, the largest Iranian-American advocacy group." (2).

Part of it is to expand access to information and communications through the internet for Iranians."

Some readers of my book will say that I am against Jews. I am not. If you want to be an American, then you must assimilate into our society. There is no God. Prove there is.

Zionist are pushing their controlled media, the U.S. Congress, the White House, and some State Governments to make your religion your nationality. Should their efforts be accomplished, first and foremost, the U.S. Constitution would have to be eliminated as the founding document of the great country. However, equally troublesome should they succeed. We will become a country like Iraq and Saudi Arabia. Maybe you would like a religion reminder to whack your legs with a switch to remind you to go pray.

Comments

The information that I wrote was based on more than thirty five years of constant learning and research. My sources were newspapers in the Middle East and Southeast Asia, plus unclassified military documents. Domestically, I reviewed World Books, National Geographic stories, History Channel documentaries, World Almanacs, and any publication that I could find and read about the places I had been, and the people I had met. The world is a great place. Please keep the religious zealots and political prostitutes out of our lives.

Speaking of History Channel documentaries. Several months ago, I rented a DVD from Blockbuster. The title, of this made for the History Cannel documentary, was "Exodus Decoded."

Allegedly, four years of research were expended on the documentary. The producer was Mr. James Cameron.

For those of us that have sought the truth regarding the Biblical tales of God's direct intervention to make the Hebrews (individuals of Judaism), God's Chosen People, and granting Canaan (Palestine) to the Hebrews. The film debunks that Bible version of the Exodus (If in fact there was one).

The director and producer went to great lengths to show events like the Nile turning red, the Egyptian first born dying, boils, plus other plagues brought against Pharaoh, were in fact, the acts of nature (The planet evolving). For example, the plagues identified became a reality, exactly like what was written in Exodus, in the African country of Cameroon. The viewer of the film see visual proof of what nature can, did, and continues to do. One should not be amazed as volcano eruptions, earthquakes, shifting of the earth's plates, and other natural acts that affect our planet, occur each day.

Yes of course, individuals like Jerry Falwell, Pat Robertson James Dobson, and multitudes of ministers will declare that the events/ discoveries were the act of God. Truth for the ministers could eliminate or decrease the millions of dollars that they receive annually, preaching lies to Americans. Too many in the Bible Belt adore individuals of wealth, and fabricators of the truth. Look at the mentally unstable, former President George W. Bush. Bush ordered a Religious Crusade against Islam and Saddam Hussein.

For those citizens of the Red States and religious zealots, I would like to address the "Treaty of Peace and Friendship between the United States and the Bey, and Subjects of Tripoli of Barbary." The Senate ratified, and President John Adams signed the treaty for the United States on June 7, 1797.

The following is the complete text of Article 11 of said treaty. "As the Government of the United States of America is not, in any sense, founded on the Christian religion; as it has in itself no character of enmity against the laws, religion, or tranquility, of Mussulmen; and, as the said States never entered into any war, or act of hostility against an Mahometan nation, it is declared by the parties, that no pretext arising from religious opinions, shall ever produce an interruption of the harmony existing between the two countries."

We have a great nation, but unless a national referendum is placed on a national ballot soon, we will disappear as a viable nation. The referendum needed would ask the people:

(1). Is the United States of America responsible for the economic and physical security of the Socialist Country of Israel?

(2). Will the American people allow the U.S. Government to continue classifications of individuals, whose religion is Judaism, as Jews?

Normally, I suppose one would close by stating "God Bless America", but since there is no God, I would be the same as the Zionist in the Congress of the United States of America - A TRAITOR.

The Future
Peace For The United States Of America

I'll be sixty six years old on September 21, 2009. My death is in the near future. I departed the Kingdom of Laos in January 1973 with a diminished mental and physical profile. I was fortunate that I did not have to spend any nights at the Moung Soui airstrip as this site was in the heart of communist controlled territory. One American Army officer was killed and his enlisted assistant wounded during a sapper attack at the Moung Soui village or township.

During the years of the assignment, I did visit all the Joint/USAF/Army Lima Sites. I remember, for sure, remaining overnight at Luang Prabang, the Royal Capital of Laos, and I believe either Pakse or Savannakhet. Maybe both. (My memory is failing due to the shrinking of my brains frontal lobes.) Returning from my visit to the American community's most secretive site, Long Tieng, the airspace outside the aircraft began to become spotted with grayish clouds. I tapped the pilot on the shoulder and asked what the objects were. No response. He gained altitude and proceeded south to Vientiane. (The pilot attained the rank of General (four stars) prior to his retirement.)

Although I was not wounded, my back, neck and left leg were re-injured when the vehicle I was driving was hit by a Laotian driven vehicle. I was stopped in the traffic lane with my left turn signal flashing, indicating I was turning in to the Royal Laotian Headquarter's training area.

Occasionally I think to myself, "was the vehicle strike an accident or was the driver a Pathet Lao soldier or pro-communist individual that knew I was an American?" The only visible sign of the accident was the rear of my vehicle rammed in and blood from my left knee to my foot.

In my opinion, the heaviest contact of herbicide and/or foreign substance exposure occurred when I was on temporary duty to Moung Soui Airstrip, Laos. The period was June to August, 1969. Not only were we the recipients of whatever was in the air and soil at the site, we were hit by the Monsoon rains and thunderstorms originating over South Vietnam and Cambodia. The Rubber Plantations in Cambodia were a primary target for the Ranch Hand C-123 aircraft spraying Agent Orange and other toxins. Sprays in South Vietnam were to deny sanctuary for communist forces using jungle foliage as cover.

In 1993, my health started to deteriorate. My breast started leaking some type fluid. A knot had to be surgically removed from the center of my tongue. One health care provider was concerned that I might have AIDS. (I knew I had never hand any type sexual contact with anyone except for a female. Also, to my knowledge, the only blood transfusions was at the Homestead Air Force Base Hospital, Florida in 1963. An AIDS test was given with negative results.) My auto-immune systems was out of balance. The Thyroid gland was not functioning properly. My lymph nodes began swelling throughout my body similar to the outbreaks when I was in Laos. I was not only becoming a physical wreck, but, I was going down hill mentally.

Today, I am 90% service connected with a Permanent and Total Disability rating. July 18, 2009, I received a denial letter from the Department of Veterans Affairs regarding my claim for Chronic obstructive pulmonary disease due to asbestos exposure and or toxin such as Agent Orange (previously claimed as COPD, also claimed as residuals of pneumonia-previously denied as tightness in chest and shortness of breath related to Agent Orange.) Also denied, Diabetes mellitus type II to include as Secondary to Agent Orange exposure associated with herbicide exposure. ((Years past, I was diagnosed with peripheral neuropathy prior to the onset of Type II diabetes mellitus. CAT Scan/MRI reveal Right Maxilluary Sinus Disease, clogging of the abdominal Aorta, enlarged prostate, joint bone disease, fractured lower spine, narrowing of the spine at the neck, damaged right shoulder and wrist plus traumatic arthritis. (The ailments listed is only a partial listing.) Decade long diseases include Colitis and Post Traumatic Stress Disorder.

The VA rater wrote I did indeed have the diseases identified but they had no record of me being assigned to the Republic of South Vietnam. (The 1991 Agent Orange Act (paraphrasing) - a service member had to be stationed, official orders, physically on and/or visited the country (boots on the ground) of South Vietnam during the Vietnam War era.)

I wrote a Letter of Disagreement that stated (paraphrasing): Yes, I was never in the Republic of South Vietnam but I was in the Kingdom of Laos; whereas, some of us were subjected to the same hostilities, toxin exposures, and other hazards to one's health as the American military person in South Vietnam.

How do you tell a pilots family, an aircrew members mother, and/ or special ops person's girlfriend their loved one was killed but since they were in an illegal war, survivors benefits would not be paid? For example, during one combat training sortie, the Air Operations Center Commander at Luang Prabang Lima Site was killed. A message from the U.S. State Department's (Vientiane embassy) representative was dispatched saying his survivors could not receive any government benefits because he was on an unauthorized flight. (On this tragic day, allegedly the Rules of Engagement and/or embassy policy was American pilots could not fly sorties with Laotian pilot trainees with aircraft loaded with live ordnance.) With elation, I remember reading a message from Under Secretary of State Marshall Green voiding the denial message.

I've written President Barack H. Obama, Senator Mitch McConnell, and Congressman Harold Rogers regarding the disparity between presumptive rating awards for armed forces members that served in South Vietnam and the special project members that were assigned to Cambodia and Laos on orders that read "Classified Southeast Asia Assignment." I've asked via telephone the assistance of Congressman Harold Rogers and Congressman Ben Chandler to sign as co-sponsors of HR2254. Congressman Rogers represents Kentuckians from Kentucky's 5th U.S. Congressional District which covers southern and southeast Kentucky. Congressman Chandler's district is Central Kentucky - the Blue Grass Region. (To date they have not.)

For the unfamiliar HR2254 now reads for those military members that served in the vicinity of Vietnam. If approved this amendment to the 1991 Agent Orange Act would allow veterans exposed to Agent Orange or other toxins the same presumptive rating ability as the boots on the ground Vietnam veteran.

Another question. If someone actually read this book, they may say who gives a shit about the denial of Veterans Administration medical and monetary benefits, especially for a disease that is going to kill and/or hasten the death of the veteran?

The answer my fellow American, is that, if the government denies those of us dispatched to a classified war zone, without the knowledge or consent of Congress; then one must logically think our government will deny those veterans from the wars with Iraq and Afghanistan.

Moreover with all due respect to former service members that served in Indo-China and Thailand during the Vietnam War era; military personnel from the Kuwait - Iraq conflict plus the thousands that have been at war in Iraq and Afghanistan, since 2003, will suffer a greater number of mental and physical ailments than the Vietnam era veteran.

The reasons are: depleted uranium munitions, transiting through radioactive terrain, non-properly purified water, house to house fighting and the Improvised Explosive Devices (IED). (A recent research conclusion was that 52 % of military veterans from Iraq and Afghanistan will suffer Traumatic Brain Injury (TBI). However, what makes the medical situation worse is that more of those injured will not be returning to military bases but to their hometowns. The use of National Guardsman and Reserve Forces will have a negative effect on the population of the United States of America and her citizens.

The reader and I both know, the Congress of the United States will continue to cower to large corporations and the so-called religious community (Zionist and Old Testament Christians). Therefore, U.S. Forces will continue to be used as pawns to provide U.S. and Israeli Corporations with assess to fossil fuels and/or any commodity sought. (As former President Dwight David Eisenhower warned that nation about the U.S. Military Industrial Complex, the powerful on Wall Street and the U.S. Congress are keeping defense contractors in the money.)

And, am I the only one is the Commonwealth of Kentucky concerned about Zionist? For example, individuals of Judaism have been killing historically their Arab cousins for centuries in the name of the same God. (All three major religions from Palestine and Arabia's God is the God of Abraham.) In the United States our war, with those of Islam, began in 1948 when former President Harry Truman, a Christian Zionist, recognized the illegal announcement of statehood by Jewish terrorist in the land of Palestine.

I suppose individuals are fed up with my written and verbal words regarding the control of the United States Government by Jews and Old Testament Christians. The United States is a Republic, not a Theocracy style of government. For myself, I do not care who or what is your religious entity. Worship as you like but do not involve my country in a religious crusade until you can prove there is a God and that entity orders the United States to wage war against Islam at the threat of total destruction. Until that day, cease and detest you subversive acts against the United States Government.

Keeping with my thought and words, President Thomas Jefferson wrote there would be times for Americans to rise up and replace the government with a new government. (The time is long overdue.) We the people must vote out all incumbents in Congress in 2010 and 2012 plus remove Vice President Joseph Biden, Zionist, from office as was former Vice President Spiro Agnew. Failure to do so will result in the same environment as pre-World War II Germany.

Peace is attainable for all mankind.

Billy Ray Wilson

209 Autumn Drive

London, KY 40744-7071

(606) 862-2847 phone

(606) 330-0124

August 8, 2009

Project 404 members, RAVENS, 56th SOW Maintenance, and the United States Embassy Staff Vientiane, Laos.

SUBJECT: In Tribute and an Appeal

Dear Americans:

THE TRIBUTE

This letter is to thank those individuals and families I worked with in the Kingdom of Laos from September 1968 to January 1973.

No! I was not a RAVEN, from the 56th SOW or a USAF person attached to the United States Central Intelligence Agency. I was an air force enlisted person attached to the U.S. Embassy's Air Attache Office, Vientiane, Laos.

I entered Laos after in-processing at the Capital Hotel, Bangkok, Thailand. At the hotel, I left my military status behind and became a U.S. Forest Worker attached to the Air Attache's Office. Laos was a classified Southeast Asia location at the time.

Over the next four years and few months, my duties were in the Air Attache's Command & Control Center in the old and new Air Attache Building. However, in truth, I was still an air force enlisted my duties were at the pleasure of the Air Attache and the United States Ambassador to Laos.

One could not write or speak about the Laotian Air War without addressing the RAVENS, 56th SOW personnel, Combined Air Support staff, the Ambassador and his staff, and, of course, the U.S. Governments AID to Laos. To this end, the organizations and individuals identified accomplished more militarily than the 500 thousand U.S. Military personnel assigned to the Republic of South Vietnam.

The death toll was high among the RAVENS. A couple of AOC Commanders were killed. One by enemy fire and the second crashed into the Mekong River, in the Vientiane area. Cause unknown. An enlisted person was receiving an orientation ride from the AOC Commander. (A short time after the crash, a Laotian farmer brought in remains of one of the individuals from the second crash. The embassy allegedly paid him $50.00.)

In my opinion, the majority of assigned U.S. Military, whether legal or illegal accomplished our tasks to the best of our abilities. Yes, there were some in Laos getting their tickets punched for better promotion chances and others for their own reasons. At first, I truly believed in what we were doing but by the time I was ready to come home I was disillusioned.

Regarding the RAVENS and the special operations personnel that gave all they had and more; I am proud to have worked with you.

THE APPEAL

The assignment in Laos, followed by the assignment to the Joint Casualty Resolution Center approximately six months later, changed my life. War should be the last resolution choice.

Since those of us that were assigned to the major cities, with operational runways, we lived on the economy. We were part of the Laotian community.

In this status, we spoke with the different nationalities residing in or transient in Laos. You had a French community outside the city of Vientiane from the days Laos was a colony. Cambodians, Vietnamese, Chinese, Hmoung (Meo), Thai, for whatever their reasons for being in Laos, to the person, did not want the United States Government interfering in their lives. (The Saudis had the same opinion. The people, like in Indo-China respected the American people but disliked the government of the United States.

As a military person, regardless of rank, each of us swore an oath to defend and uphold the U.S. Constitution against all enemies foreign and domestic. The hours we spent in a base theatre being lectured on the punishment one would receive for disobeying or violating one of the articles of the Uniform Code of Military Justice (USMJ) should be revisited.

One may forget many of the article numbers but surely a person would remember the article the dictates one does not have to follow an order if that order is unlawful in accordance with the UCMJ.

For the purpose of this letter, let us return to the date President

Thomas Jefferson sent the Navy to rescue Americans in Libya. Too me, President Jefferson properly used the U.S. Navy to assure international commerce. The Constitution dictates the government will regulate commerce. You can not regulate commerce when the seaways are threatened. Today, the government not only has the seaways but the air routes and land transportation avenue to keep free of aggressive parties.

Some years after Robert E. Lee graduated from West Point, he was in charge of a military unit that was instrumental in capturing the abolitionist John Brown. Of more recent history, our military has been used to assure the civil rights of all Americans.

In my opinion, the only war in my lifetime that has been justified is World War II. Japan bombed the U.S. Naval Base at Pearl Harbor, Hawaii. However, according to a number of publications and documentaries, President Roosevelt and our government instigated the war with Japan. Most likely the large corporations and Wall Street money lenders were behind our aggressive tactics.

Don't read me wrong. The United States must maintain military superiority in the international community to assure the security of the United States and her territories. The military must be capable of assuring commerce avenues are open and safe for the import and export of international trade. Military leaders must make resignation from their hard earned status in their applicable service a major factor to assure the Congress of the United States of America does not take our great nation in to a theocracy state. The United States of America is the foundation of this great nation. Equally important, the Declaration of Independence says it all - we are all equals.

Please if you love the United States of America, then you should put the United States first in your lives. Religious entities and Gods have come and gone throughout the centuries. If you were born in the United States or naturalized through the U.S. Department of Justice Department, then you are an American.

Make international peace possible.

MY FELLOW AMERICANS & PRESIDENT GEORGE W. BUSH

We are a nation of 300 million individuals, of which not all are religious, especially me. For you, President Bush, to invoke God for war against the sovereign country of Iraq should be reviewed by the Congress of the United States of America. The United States is a Republic, not a Theocracy.

To underscore what I wrote above, please read below, a quote, published in the Louisville Courier-Journal Newspaper, January 7, 2007. The title of the column was: "What would they do about Iraq?" The writer of the column was author Mr. Harold Holzer. The they were: Julius Caesar, George Washington, Genghis Khan, and Abraham Lincoln.

Mr. Holzer: "Abandon the notion of divine will to justify war. Even the pious Lincoln came to realize it was fruitless, even sacrilegious, to invoke God as his ally." Mr. Lincoln "In great contests each party claims to act in accordance with the will of God. "Lincoln lamented. "Both may be, and one must be, wrong." As Lincoln understood: "The Almighty has his own purposes."

ABRAHAM LINCOLN

"In great contests each party claims to act in accordance with the will of God." "Both may be, and one must be wrong." "The Almighty has his own purposes."

POPE

"An atheist is but a mad ridiculous derider of piety; but a hypocrite makes a sober jest of God and religion; he finds it easier to be upon his knees than to rise to a good action."

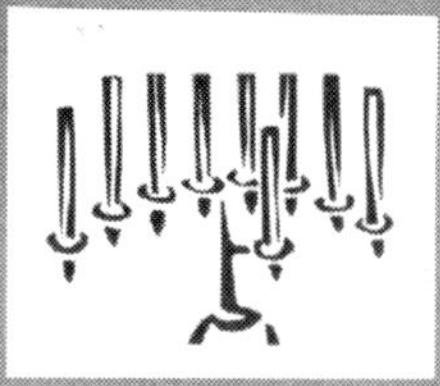

"No man SHALL be compelled to frequent or support any religious worship, place, or ministry whatsoever, nor shall be enforced, restrained, molested, or burdened in his body or goods, nor shall otherwise suffer, on account of his religious opinion or belief; but that all men shall be free to profess, and by argument to maintain, their opinions in matters of religion, and that same shall in no wise diminish, enlarge, or affect their civil capabilities."

THOMAS JEFFERSON 3RD President of the United States of America

BILLY RAY WILSON FOR CONGRESS, REPUBLICAN

KENTUCKY'S FIFTH U.S. CONGRESSIONAL DISTRICT

Right away, I know I may offend many with my candid words, but I stand with the Declaration of Independence, the Constitution of the United States of America and our country's Bill of Rights. The individuals that came from different countries of the international community arrived in North America after considerable hardships for multiple reasons but most, in my opinion, came seeking the freedoms that we so cherish described in the Declaration of Independence. Yet, the current parties are taking this great nation back to the Europe of the 1600s; however, regrettably, there are no new countries to explore and establish a nation of the people, by the people, and for the people. Our only recourse is to replace the Federal Executive and Legislative Branches with Americans in 2004 and 2006. The two elections could replace the entire U.S. Government and, hopefully, take our country back on the track envisioned by our founders.

My fellow citizens of the Commonwealth of Kentucky and the Republic of the United States of America, I will provide a quote by, in my opinion, a founding friend of our Commonwealth and the greatest President of the United States of America – Thomas Jefferson.

"How soon the labor of man would make a paradise of the whole earth, were it not for misgovernment, and a diversion of all his energies from their proper object – the happiness of man – to the selfish interest of kings, nobles and priests."

– Thomas Jefferson to Ellen W. Collidge, 1825

Using the words "kings, nobles and priests" from the last quote, one can apply the words Chief Executive Officers (CEO), Members of Congress and Zionist/Christian clergy in their stead. The CEOs, both civil and federal, have changed from serving in the best interest of the people of the United States and the United States herself to their stockholders and self-interest. Members of Congress are utilizing the honorable chambers of the U.S. House and Senate to instill discord among the American people and destroy our nation from within through covert and overt support of their religious and ancestral heritage. (For example, as of March 9, 2004, five hundred fifty-four American military personnel have been killed and several thousand severely wounded because of the cited Congressional Action.) The Zionist/Christian clergy are perpetrating the greatest hoax, in my opinion, on the American people that ever plagued the civilized world -- unproven religious prophesy.

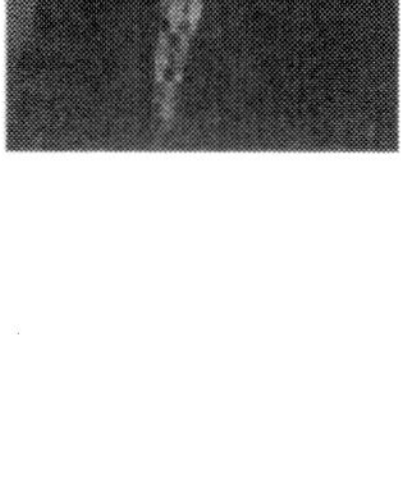

Moreover, Americans have the right to worship or not to worship whatever God or entity he or she chooses to as the Constitution stipulates. (Our country has no state religion.) For myself, religion should be a private affair with one's own religious entity and, in my opinion, a person should live their lives in accordance with their chosen religious teachings; then the non-believers could approach them based on day to day observations of the person's religious stature.

On May 18, 2004, I ask for your vote to replace the honorable Harold (Hal) Rogers, R-Somerset, as Kentucky's Fifth U.S. Congressional District's Member of the U.S. House of Representatives. If you believe the Constitution stipulates the district's Washington representative is to solicit un-funded budget dollars for Eastern Kentucky, then you should vote for Congressman Rogers. But, you should know, the representative is in Washington to protect state's rights, regulate commerce and protect the United States of America from domestic and foreign enemies; therefore, you should vote for me. I will make no promises other than my life will be served in the people's interest, not the Republican Party or special interest.

NOTE: Should the reader wish to address their concerns or questions in person, you may schedule a question and answer session in your county and I will attend. If you do not want to meet in person, then you may write, fax, telephone or send an e-mail message to the addresses and numbers identified at the bottom of this political advertisement.

This political message is paid for by the Billy Ray Wilson Campaign for Congress
209 Autumn Ridge Drive, London, KY 40744-7071
Telephone (606) 862-2847
Fax (606) 862-2847
e-mail brwilson04@adelphia.net

ECONOMIC IMPROVEMENT IDEAS

The physical location of Laurel County and the remaining twenty-eight counties of Kentucky's Fifth Congressional District could provide our nation with enhanced postal distribution, travel related business, recreational activities, new agriculture crops for the nation, and with extremely well educated, morally enlightened, stable, and talented Kentuckians ready to enter the workforce. Therefore, based on the probable vocational areas identified, the following are a few examples of letters I have written to promote our region:

1 Recommend to former Governor Paul Patton the authorization of local high schools to establish an in-school employment office for graduating high school students. The office would coordinate with local, county, state, federal employment offices and fortune five hundred companies to establish an annual Job's Fair within a school district or larger geographical area that would open up the nation and the international community for employment opportunities. Likewise, the state and local municipalities may want to assist those students unable to attend college or universities with monetary assistance to relocate to an employment site should the potential employer not provide relocation expenses.

2 Recommended to Senator Mitch McConnell for the U.S. Postal Service to open a central mail distribution center at the London-Corbin Airport due to our hub location on Interstate 75 and the projected Interstate 66 that would provide faster and more efficient mail distribution to cities and townships located North, East, South and West of the distribution center. Likewise, the London area has better weather and less traffic congestion than the cities now breaking down the mail for interstate distribution. Senator McConnell forwarded my letter to the United States Postal Service for review.

3 Recommended to Kentucky's Agriculture Department to seek information from the United Nations regarding a new strain of rice developed during the Air War in Indo-China for use by the hill tribesmen of Southeast Asia. Based on what I learned through hearsay, the new rice strain should thrive in our mountains as it, allegedly, does in the mountains of Laos, Philippines, and Thailand.

4 A couple of years past, I advocated re-introducing Hemp to replace tobacco as a cash crop for our region. (As you may or may not know, Hemp was once a thriving money crop in Kentucky.) A former member of the United States House of Representatives told me the crop would not be viable as Congress would have to establish a Hemp subsidy as they have for so many of the other agriculture products. To his response, my answer is that there will always be a need for rope products plus the numerous other products that can now be made from Hemp. (For the un-informed, Hemp is not an intoxicating drug that so many seek and sought from Marijuana.)

5 With the installation of an Instrument Landing System (ILS) and extension of London-Corbin's Airport, our community will over the next decade and beyond provide air cargo services, scheduled air service, and air charter services with a large runway that's operational twenty-four hours a day with all weather airport landing/take off capabilities in which to service the local region and points to the North, South, East, and West. Our new era in aviation will bring an unknown number of jobs and opportunities for the people of Southeastern and Eastern Kentucky.

6 A more recent proposal to both state and federal elected officials dealt with building a light rail commuter System parallel with Interstate 75 from Cincinnati to the Tennessee border and possibly on to Knoxville, Tennessee. Spur routes would be built into Eastern Kentucky to afford our citizens the ability to travel to and from their residences to work centers located in Central and Northern Kentucky and commute to schools, Department of Veterans Affairs Medical Centers and other equally important destinations for Kentuckians. Our region of the country will only grow through the over-population of the major cities and industrial areas. We need to look forward, not to the past. Our region has the resources and will to make life better for our future generations.

We the people of Kentucky and the United States need to replace those in Washington with loyalties to their religion and land of their ancestry with Americans. This great land of ours belongs to the people and not to the nobles, kings, clergy and those believing themselves to be a chosen people. In the United States of America, we are all Americans.

The first photograph (above) reveals an Anti-Aircraft Artillery (AAA) site somewhere in Laos. The picture below is both historically and ancient of stone jars found on the Plane de Jares in Northern Laos.

GEOFFREY CLIFFORD

Photographs of my first wife and I getting married at the Homestead Air Force Base Chapel in April 1964. I still remember my Mississippi friend and best man asking me "are you sure?" I told him I had no choice.

Photographs of me ranging in years from a baby to graduating from Air Force Base Training.

My mother, older sister, and me sitting in front of Grandmother Brown's home.

Great Grandfather Green Chandler & Great Grandmother Louisa Belvin Chandler.
My Grandmother Lear Chandler not shown in this photograph.

Great Grandfather Samuel Casteel.

My second wife and I cutting our wedding cake at Poro Point, Republic of the Philippines.

Photo Courtesy of Charles F. Printz

A memorial stone at Arlington National Cemetery for the Lao and Hmong killed in Laos supporting U.S. Foreign Policy. Their actions, along with American Advisors, kept Communist Forces on the offensive which provided longer longevity for the South Vietnamese Government. When Laos became Communist in 1973, South Vietnam fell in 1975.

A-7 Corsair II (replacement Search & Rescue
Aircraft for the A-1E Skyraiders)

A-1E Sky raiders (Probably the best aircraft ever built for insurgency or jungle warfare plus Search & Rescue Missions.)

AC-130 Gunship
Call Sign: SPECTRE

AC-47 Spooky

0-1 Bird Dog
assigned to the
U.S. Army

Call Sign: STINGER

AC-119 gunship

The picture above depicts unity while the lower picture reveals the true Lao. The Communist won because of their sponsors not because of the support of the majority of the Laotian people. The people only wanted to live in peace to raise their families.

Photo by Dong Muang Royal Thai Air Base of President Lyndon B. Johnson and Lady Bird Johnson during their visit with the King and Queen of Thailand.

Receiving an Air Force Commendation Medal from the U.S. Air Attache, Vientiane,
Great Grandfather Samuel Casteel.

The two aircraft identified in this photograph were among the military resources provided by the U.S. Government to the Kingdom of Laos during President Dwight David Eisenhower's administration. The top aircraft was the T-28 which was the type of aircraft the Air Operations Center Commander at Luang Prabang was Killed. The 0-1 Bird dog below was the war machine in which too many American and Laotian pilots and/or back seat advisors were killed.

Interesting note regarding an incident involving an internationally known journalist. For years, the international news media wanted to visit the agencies primary forward operating location (FOL) in Laos. The U.S. Embassy agreed and flew a number of journalist to Sam Thong, Laos (near the primary FOL.) The troublesome, former British Special Services journalist broke away from the group and attempted to make his way to the FOL on foot. He was captured. Had it not been for the case officer at the FOL, the journalist would be dead.

These photos depict the total U.S. Mission to Laos (above) and the facilities used by those fighting

Communist countries that contributed different type of war resources to the Pathet Lao.

I learned from two different media sources of the 1975 refugee airlift from Long Tieng, what I don't understand, why were the Ravens included in people to be evacuated? I was in Vientiane, the latter part of 1973 and the first quarter of 1974; the Pathet Lao had already taken control of Vientiane.

The aircraft to the left is the Platius Porter. This aircraft was used to transport General Vang Pao during his economic and military dealings in the kingdom. (Remember the movie "Air America?)

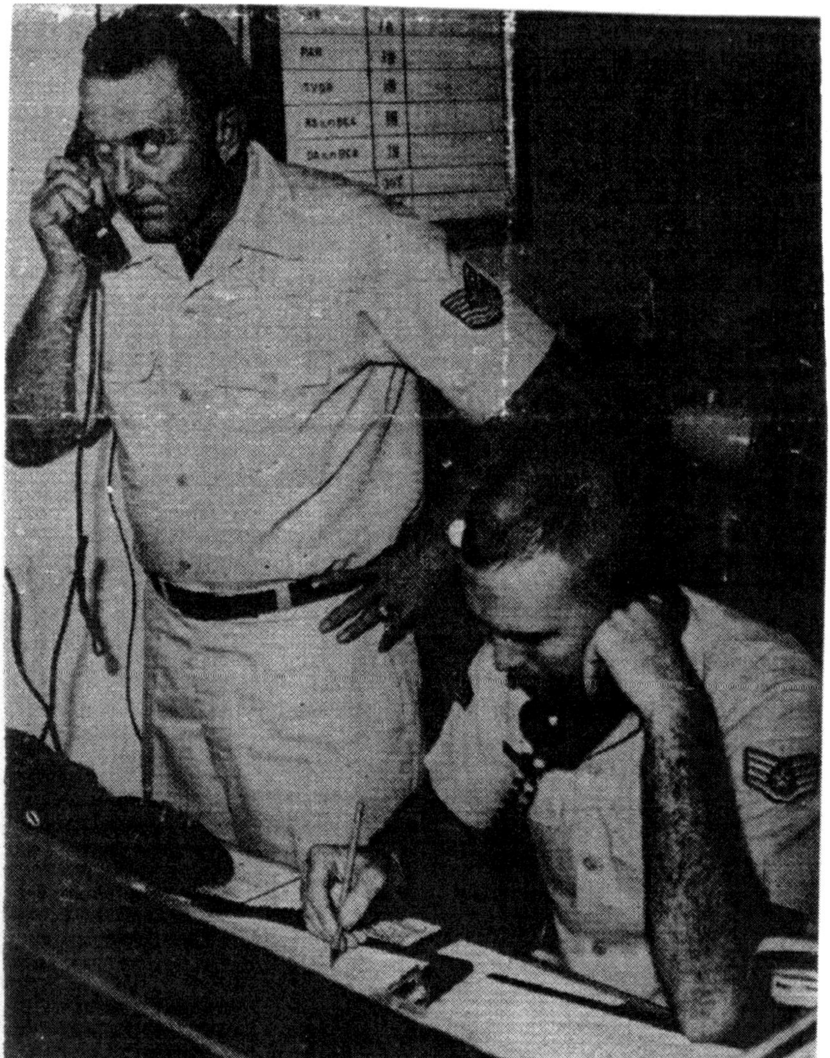

"Clear To Land" . . . Giving landing instructions to A
Force One is MSgt. Warren F. Whitby, (left) 49, of Highland, Cali
and SSgt. Billy R. Wilson, 23 of London, Ky.

The top aircraft is a F-4 (workhorse of the Vietnam War). The middle photo is of an AC-130 Gunship. The combination of these two aircraft diverted to sites under siege like Long Tieng, saved many American and allies lives.

The RB-57 Aircraft, in Vietnam, were flown by both U.S. and Australian pilots. I recall from intell sources of an Australian aircrew flying a RB-57 being shot down, capture, and the long march to Hanoi.

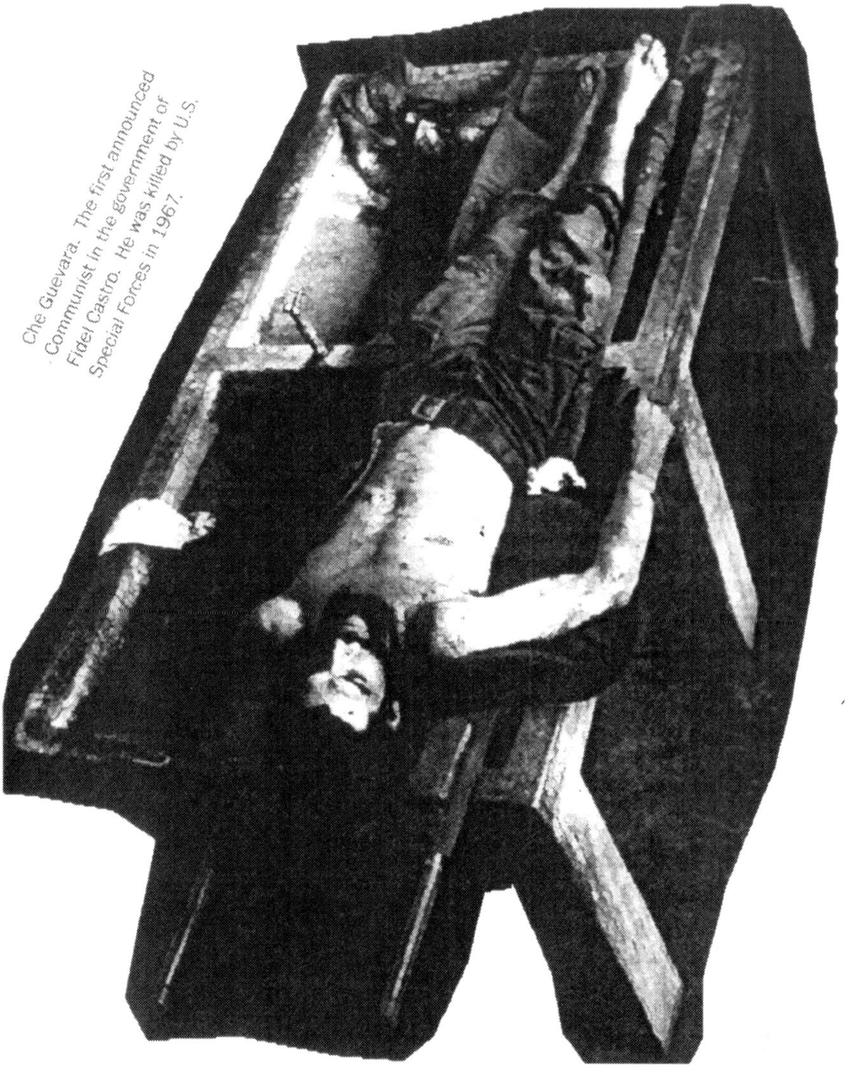

Che Guevara. The first announced Communist in the government of Fidel Castro. He was killed by U.S. Special Forces in 1967.

Pictured are my ex-wife Linda Warren and myself at our wedding reception.

PROCE
WITH

THE "SECRET WAR" IN LAOS

In Memorial to the following Ravens:

Wayne T. Abbey
Robert L. Abbott
Henry L. Allen
John J. Bach
Charles D. Ballou
Danny L. Berry
Frank Tifton Birk
Park George Bunker
Joseph K. Bush Jr.
John Leonard Carroll
Joseph L. Chestnut
James E. Cross
Daniel Richard Davis
Richard H. Defer
Samuel M. Deichelmann
David A. Dreier
Richard G. Elzinga
Charles E. Engle
Stanley L. Erstad
Robert E. Foster
Jerry D. Furche
John J. Garritty
Melville D. Hart
Richard Walter Herold
Paul Vernon Jackson III
Charles Larimore Jones

John J. Keeler
William Joseph Kozma
Edward E. McBride
Paul A. Merrick
Harold Louis Mischler
Dennis Edward Morgan
Donald Craig Morrison
Steven J. Neal
Andrew L. Patten
Richard Brooks Patterson
Joseph W. Potter
Gomer David Reese III
Dale F. Richardson
James Rostermundt
M.E. (Russ) Roussell
Charles P. Russell
Larry Kent Sanborn
Don W. Service
Prescott N. Shinn
Richard E. Shubert
Marlin Lynn Siegwalt
Michael Lewis Stearns
George Henry Tousley III
Willis Grant Uhls
John A. Webb
John W. White III
James R. Withers
James A. Yeager
Truman R. Young

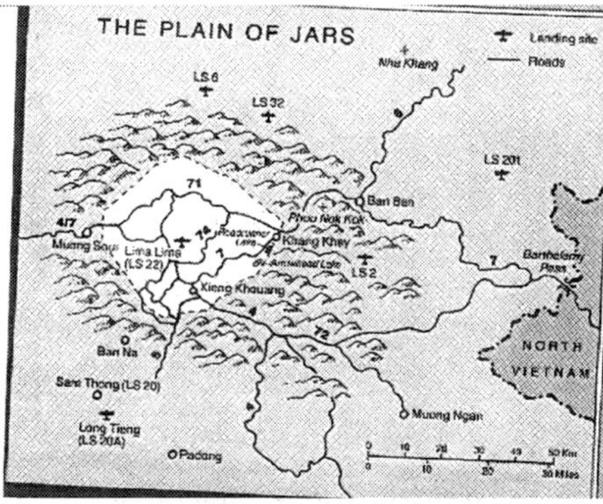
THE PLAIN OF JARS
Landing site
Roads
Nha Khang
LS 6
LS 32
LS 201
Ban Ban
Phou Nok Kok
Muong Soui
Lima Lima (LS 22)
Khang Khay
LS 2
Xieng Khouang
Barthelemy Pass
NORTH VIETNAM
Ban Na
Sam Thong (LS 20)
Long Tieng (LS 20A)
Muong Ngan
Padong
50 Km
30 Miles

348014

Jim Roper photo from Laos

R F R

USA

Breinigsville, PA USA
12 September 2010
245278BV00001B/62/P

9 781449 056919